TOGETHER

TOGETHER

OUR COMMUNITY COOKBOOK

THE HUBB COMMUNITY KITCHEN

PHOTOGRAPHY BY
JENNY ZARINS

Clarkson Potter/Publishers
New York

Dedication

This book is dedicated to all those whose lives
were impacted by the fire at Grenfell Tower.

CONTENTS

FOREWORD

Together is more than a cookbook. This is a tale of friendship, and a story of togetherness. It is a homage to the power of cooking as a community, and the recipes that allow us to connect, share and look forward.

In January 2018, as I was settling in to my new home of London, it was important to me to get to know organizations working in the local community. I made a quiet trip to Al-Manaar, a mosque close to the Grenfell community.

In 2017, I had watched the Grenfell Tower tragedy unfold on the news; I was in Canada at the time, sharing the global sentiment of shock and sympathy for what this community was enduring, while also deeply wanting to help. Fast-forward seven months, and I was set to meet some of the women affected by the fire, at a community kitchen in Al-Manaar.

The kitchen was opened after the Grenfell tragedy, offering women who had been displaced and the community around them a space to cook food for their families. Their roles as matriarchs united them across their cultures; the kitchen provided an opportunity to cook what they knew and to taste the memory of home, albeit homes some had recently lost.

The kitchen buzzes with women of all ages; women who have lived and seen life; laughing, chatting, sharing a cup of tea and a story, while children play on the floor or are rocked to sleep in their strollers. Now I have come to know these women and this place well, here are a few things to note about the community kitchen:

It is cozy and brightly lit, with scents of cardamom, curry
and ginger dancing through the air.

It will take you about fifteen minutes to enter the room, as you will be joyfully greeted
by kisses (cheek x 3) by each of the incredible women there.

You will find yourself in a melting pot of cultures and personalities, who have roots
in Uganda, Iraq, Morocco, India, Russia and at least ten other countries.

You should undoubtedly arrive on an empty stomach because upon departure
you will have been stuffed to the gills with samosas flecked with cinnamon, chapatis
flavored with carrots and onion, Russian semolina cake, Persian teas and my very
favorite avocado dip that I now make at home.

You will feel joyful in their company, and you will leave counting
the days until you go back.

On my first visit, I asked Munira, the resident *chef de cuisine* (so to speak), how I could help. An apron was quickly wrapped around me, I pushed up my sleeves, and I found myself washing the rice for lunch. Munira's sister-in-law, who had flown in from Egypt after Grenfell to assist the family, helped me divide the correct amount of butter and fresh thyme to pour into the pot of rice bubbling away on the stovetop. All the aromas percolating in a kitchen filled with countless languages aflutter remains one of my most treasured memories from my first visit to the kitchen.

I have a lifelong interest in the story of food – where it comes from, why we embrace it and how it brings us together: the universal connection to community through the breaking of bread. Within this kitchen's walls, there exists not only the communal bond of togetherness through sharing food, but also a cultural diversity that creates what I would describe as a passport on a plate: the power of a meal to take you to places you've never been, or transport you right back to where you came from.

One of my own favorite meals is collard greens, black-eyed peas and cornbread – a meal I would look forward to throughout my childhood: the smell of yellow onions simmering among a slow-cooked pot of greens from my grandma's back garden; the earthy texture of peas; and a golden loaf of cornbread puff-puffing away to a browned peak in the warmth of the oven. This was always eaten on New Year's Day, a tradition steeped in ancestral history in which each component has a meaning: the black-eyed peas for prosperity, the greens for wealth, the cornbread for health and nourishment. It wasn't a New Year's resolution; it was a wish. It wasn't simply a meal; it was a story.

I've spent many years away from my birthplace of Los Angeles and have found that traveling far from home highlights the power of personally meaningful recipes. During my time at university in Chicago I would wait with bated breath to return to LA for the winter break and have a bowl of my mother's gumbo. And while living in Toronto (seven years of being adopted by that beautiful place for work), I embraced poutine and several other Canadian culinary favorites, but the Southern California girl in me always craved fish tacos, and the memory of eating hometown fare infused with a strong Mexican influence.

We've all had that experience where you have a bite of food, close your eyes, and taste, remember and even feel the first time you enjoyed it. There is good reason that chicken soup is often credited with healing not just a cold, but the soul. There is something quintessentially restorative about a taste of something meaningful.

I immediately felt connected to this community kitchen; it is a place for women to laugh, grieve, cry and cook together. Melding cultural identities under a shared roof, it creates a space to feel a sense of normalcy – in its simplest form, the universal need to connect, nurture and commune through food, through crisis or joy – something we can all relate to.

During my visit I met Zahira, a working mom who oversees much of the coordination at Al-Manaar and whose infectious smile is enough to make you forget any troubles. Upon learning the kitchen was only open on Tuesdays and Thursdays I asked, "Why isn't this open seven days a week?"

Her response: "Funding."

And now just a few months later, here we are… Together.

Through this charitable endeavor, the proceeds will allow the kitchen to thrive and keep the global spirit of community alive. With the support of dynamic women from all walks of life, we have come together with a united vision to empower other women to share their stories through food. This cookbook is a celebration of life, community and the impact of coming together.

Our hope is that within these pages you will find new recipes and family favorites that you can enjoy in your own homes, because these recipes aren't simply meals; they are stories of family, love, of survival and of connection. From a Thanksgiving supper to a Shabbat dinner or a Sunday roast, the meals that bring us together are the meals that allow us to grow, to listen, to engage and to be present. We invite you to do the same, *together*, in your home, communities and beyond.

Great thanks to everyone who made this book possible. And thanks to you, the reader, for supporting the good work of the Hubb Community Kitchen.

Now it's time…
To gather, Together.

HRH THE DUCHESS OF SUSSEX

INTRODUCTION

Our kitchen has always been a place of good food, love, support and friendship. We cook the recipes we've grown up with; there's no stress, and the recipes always work because they have been made so many times – it's proper comfort food. Cakes, stews and spicy dips have become some of our favorite weekly dishes.

A love of cooking and sharing food brought us together after the Grenfell fire. Swapping family recipes and moments of laughter gave us a sense of normality and home. We named ourselves the Hubb Community Kitchen to celebrate the thing that we all feel every time we meet – *hubb* means "love" in Arabic.

One day in January we had a surprise visit from Meghan; she cooked with us, and asked why the kitchen was only open two days a week. We replied, "funding." We thought she was joking when she said, "Well, how about making a cookbook?" But here we are, publishing *Together*, which will help to keep the kitchen open as long as we need it.

As everyone who was affected by the fire in 2017 settles into their new lives, we will continue to share the blessings of food made with love with those around us. And we hope that other people and communities can experience the healing power of sharing food by setting up their own local kitchens.

But the thing we want most is for you to enjoy cooking these recipes at home with your families. Each dish has a story, some handed down from generation to generation. We hope that by making them, and serving them, you will weave your own stories in with ours, creating a connection across our countries and cultures.

THE WOMEN OF THE HUBB COMMUNITY KITCHEN

BREAKFASTS

SHAKSHOUKA

My father's family owned olive presses in Algeria. When he came back from business trips, he brought with him oil that was as green as grass – quite unlike anything we'd seen before. He used to make this special breakfast for us to celebrate his return. Cook peppers, tomatoes and onions, add zucchini if you like, break in some eggs and eat with flatbread. Delicious!

SERVES 4

2 tbsp olive oil
2 onions, finely chopped
2 green peppers, seeded and
    finely sliced
2 garlic cloves, minced
½ tsp cumin seeds
1 tbsp tomato paste
7 ripe tomatoes, roughly
    chopped (or 1 400g/
    14.5-oz can chopped
    tomatoes)
75ml/5 tbsp cup water
4 eggs
salt and pepper
flatbreads and Greek yogurt,
    to serve

Heat the oil in a wide pan over medium–high heat. When hot, add the onions and peppers and cook for about 10 minutes, stirring often, until soft and lightly colored.

Add the garlic and cook for 2 minutes, then add the cumin seeds and tomato paste and cook for 2 minutes until fragrant.

Add the tomatoes and water and simmer for 10 minutes or until the tomatoes have broken down and the mixture has thickened slightly. Season with salt and pepper to taste.

Make four small hollows in the mixture and crack an egg into each. Gently simmer until the egg whites are cooked, but the yolks remain runny, 15–20 minutes.

Serve from the pan, along with flatbreads and Greek yogurt.

BARLEY PORRIDGE WITH FRUIT & NUTS

My Lebanese husband is a real gym freak and likes to eat healthily, so I look for lower-fat versions of the traditional dishes from our cultures. I love anything made with couscous, so this porridge fits the bill for both of us. And you don't have to stand over a pan stirring on busy mornings. I vary the amount of milk – I prefer a firm texture, but Hussein has it more like normal porridge.

SERVES 4

150g/1 cup barley couscous
   (*belboula*)
2 tsp olive or vegetable oil
300ml/1¼ cups boiling
   water
½ tsp ground cinnamon,
   or to taste
75g/⅔ cup walnuts
150g/1 cup blueberries
75g/½ cup fresh
   pomegranate seeds
4 small figs (optional)
200ml/¾ cup milk or
   almond milk

Place the couscous in a large bowl. Add the oil and mix with a fork until all the grains are coated. Add the boiling water, cover with plastic wrap and let rest for 10 minutes. When all the water has been absorbed, fluff up the couscous with a fork and add cinnamon to taste.

To serve, pile the couscous into a large serving dish or individual bowls and smooth the surface. Decorate with walnuts, blueberries, pomegranate seeds, figs, or other toppings of your choice.

Serve the milk or almond milk on the side, to be stirred in according to taste.

MOROCCAN PANCAKES WITH HONEY & ALMOND BUTTER

I grew up in France, so to me pancakes meant delicate French crêpes. But then I discovered these delicious breakfast pancakes on a trip to my mother's homeland, Morocco. They are made without oil, so are very low in fat. *Amlou* contains argan oil – an amazing Moroccan ingredient often used in cosmetics; its unique nutty flavor makes this sweet dairy-free spread quite extraordinary. Of course, when I am short of time we have the pancakes with jam instead.

MAKES 12 PANCAKES

For the pancakes
150g/1 cup fine semolina
75g/½ cup self-raising flour
1 heaping tsp fast-acting
    dried yeast (half of a
    7g package)
½ tsp baking powder
1 tsp sugar
pinch of salt
375ml/1½ cups warm water

For the amlou *(honey and almond butter)*
¼ cup almond butter
3 tbsp honey
1 tsp culinary argan oil
    (available in health food
    stores, good supermarkets
    and online)

Put all the pancake ingredients in a large bowl and whisk well to make a smooth batter. Cover loosely with plastic wrap and let rest for about 45 minutes, until plenty of bubbles have formed and the batter has risen.

Meanwhile, put the *amlou* ingredients in a small bowl and mix with a spoon to combine; set aside.

Heat a non-stick frying pan over medium–low heat; when it's hot, add a small ladleful of batter to the pan. Cook the pancake for 3–4 minutes, until the surface has lots of bubbles and has dried. Do not flip; transfer to parchment paper and repeat with the rest of the batter, making a total of 12 pancakes. Let the pancakes cool slightly before you stack them, or they may stick together.

Serve warm, drizzled with the *amlou*.

GREEN OMELETTE

I'm a big fan of eggs for breakfast. I make this omelette filled with mushrooms and green herbs to give my two daughters a good start before a day at school. As for the cream... I can't help it. It's the Russian in me: we add cream to everything.

SERVES 4

5 tbsp unsalted butter

200g/7 oz button mushrooms, thinly sliced

16 eggs

¼ cup half-and-half or heavy cream

1 small bunch fresh chives, chopped

25g/1¼ cups fresh parsley, chopped

150g/2 cups grated Cheddar cheese

salt and pepper

Heat 1 tablespoon of the butter in a non-stick pan over medium–high heat. Add the mushrooms and cook for 4–5 minutes until golden. Transfer to a plate and set aside.

Add the eggs, half-and-half, chives, parsley and some salt and pepper to a large pitcher or mixing bowl and whisk with a fork to combine.

Heat 1 tablespoon of the butter in the same pan over medium heat. Once the butter has melted and is starting to gently sizzle, pour in a quarter of the egg mixture. Swirl the pan so the egg mixture reaches the edges and then let it cook for 5–7 minutes.

Add a quarter of the mushrooms and a quarter of the cheese to one side of the omelette. Fold the other side over the mushrooms and cheese, then cover the pan with a lid and cook for 3 minutes. Transfer to a plate and repeat the process to make four omelettes in total. Serve immediately.

AFRICAN BEIGNETS

We can all do with a little pleasure in our lives. *Mahamri* are light and fluffy buns, rather like doughnuts, and are good with cream cheese, honey or jam, although in Uganda we eat them with everything, even meat.

MAKES 12 BEIGNETS

140g/1 cup all-purpose flour, plus extra for dusting

210g/1½ cups self-rising flour

1 tsp fast-acting dried yeast (half of a 7g package)

75g/6 tbsp sugar

¼ tsp ground cardamom

1 egg, beaten

120ml/½ cup coconut milk

1 tbsp ghee, melted

1 tsp vegetable oil, plus extra for greasing

jam, honey or cream cheese, to serve

Place the flours, yeast, sugar and cardamom in a large bowl. Mix thoroughly, using your fingers.

Make a hollow in the middle of the dry ingredients and pour in the egg, coconut milk and melted ghee. Working with your fingers, gently incorporate the flour into the liquid until it comes together and forms a soft dough. Add a tablespoon of water if needed.

Knead the dough for 10 minutes, until smooth and stretchy. Rub a bit of oil between your hands and smooth this oil around the dough. Place in a lightly oiled bowl, cover with plastic wrap and leave to rise for a couple of hours, depending on the temperature of your kitchen, until doubled in size.

Preheat the oven to 400°F. Line a baking sheet with parchment paper.

Divide the dough into three equal balls. Roll each ball into a 15cm/6-inch circle, cut each circle into quarters and place them on the baking sheet. Cover with plastic wrap and let rise for 30 minutes.

Bake the beignets for 12–15 minutes, until puffed and golden. Serve with honey, jam or cream cheese, or as you prefer.

NOTE Instead of baking, you can shallow fry the beignets in sunflower oil heated to 350°F for 3–4 minutes, turning them regularly.

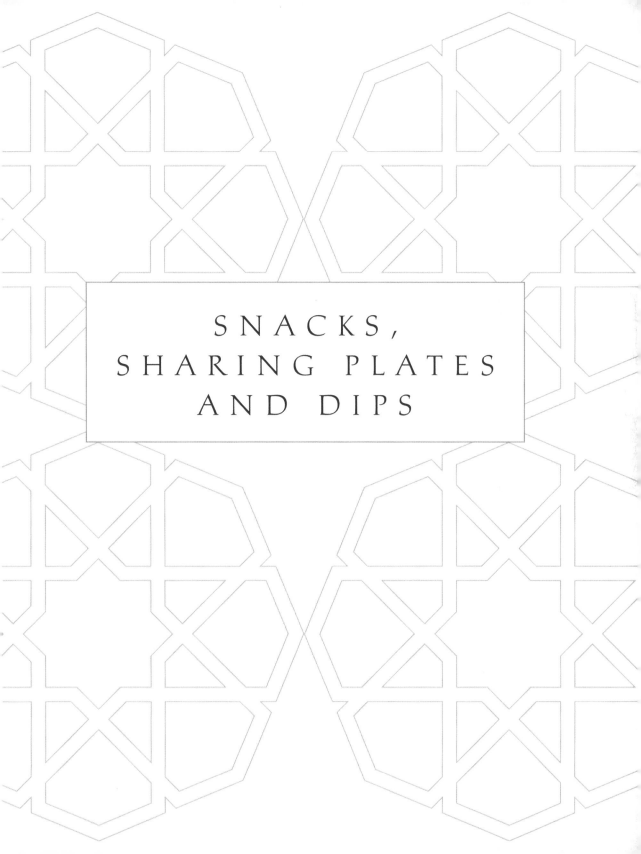

SNACKS, SHARING PLATES AND DIPS

KOFTA KEBABS WITH ONION & SUMAC PICKLE

☀ I grew up in Yemen, one of nine children. My mum's life's work was raising her family and she used to make these kebabs to fill up me and my six brothers. You can grill the kebabs or cook them in the oven – but as my mum was often in a hurry, with all those hungry growing boys, she used to quickly fry them and they would eat them straight out of the pan.

MAKES 12 KOFTAS
SERVES 4
For the Onion and
   Sumac Pickle
1 large red or yellow onion,
   halved and thinly sliced
1 tbsp white wine vinegar
½ tsp sumac (see page 90),
   plus extra to serve

For the kebabs
20g/⅓ cup breadcrumbs
3 tbsp water
1 small onion,
   roughly chopped
2 garlic cloves, peeled
10g/½ cup parsley
500g/1 lb ground beef
250g/½ lb ground lamb
1 tsp ground allspice
½ tsp ground cardamom
½ tsp sumac (see page 90)
½ tsp freshly grated nutmeg
½ tsp paprika
1 tsp salt
½ tsp freshly ground
   black pepper
vegetable oil, for brushing
pita bread and lettuce leaves,
   for serving

Soak 12 bamboo skewers (about 18cm/7 inches long) in water for 30 minutes.

To make the pickle, mix the onion slices with the vinegar in a large bowl. Sprinkle with sumac and set aside for at least 10 minutes. Sprinkle with a little more sumac when ready to serve.

Mix the breadcrumbs with the water and set aside for 5 minutes.

Put the onion, garlic and parsley in a food processor and pulse three or four times until finely chopped but not pureed. Add the beef, lamb, soaked breadcrumbs, spices, salt and pepper. Process until well mixed and paste-like.

Alternatively, if you don't have a food processor, finely chop the onion, garlic and parsley and place in a mixing bowl. Add the meat, soaked breadcrumbs and spices and knead by hand until well blended.

Divide the meat mixture into 12 portions. Mold each portion around a bamboo skewer. Place on a tray lined with parchment paper.

Heat a griddle pan over high heat until hot. Lightly brush the koftas with oil and cook for 8–9 minutes, in two batches, turning them halfway, until cooked through.

Serve with pita bread, the onion and sumac pickle and lettuce.

NOTE You can also cook the koftas on a barbecue.

EGYPTIAN LAMB FATTAH

*** My husband was born in Grenfell; his was one of the first families to move in. I learned
*** how to make this dish from his mother. It's traditional to serve it at Eid, the festival
that marks the end of Ramadan. Don't worry if you can't find gum mastic (dried resin used
as flavoring, sold in Middle Eastern shops and online); the dish works just as well without.

SERVES 4

7 tbsp melted ghee or
   vegetable oil
2 onions, roughly chopped
900g/2 lb lamb neck fillet or
   boneless lamb shoulder,
   cut into 2.5cm/1-in pieces
½ tsp gum mastic (optional)
8 cardamom pods, crushed
2 bay leaves
1 liter/1 quart chicken stock
300g/1½ cups Egyptian
   short grain rice or
   long grain rice
850ml/3½ cups water
3 pita breads
1 tbsp minced garlic
5 tbsp tomato paste
½ tsp ground cumin
1 tbsp white wine vinegar
salt and pepper

Heat 3 tablespoons of ghee or oil in a large sauté pan over medium
heat. Add the onions and cook for 5 minutes, until soft but not
golden. Add the lamb and fry for 10 minutes, until lightly browned.
Add the mastic (if using), cardamom and bay leaves, followed by
the stock. Season with salt and pepper, bring to a boil and skim off
the foam on the surface. Lower the heat, cover and gently simmer
for 1 hour (or 1½ hours if using lamb shoulder), until tender.

Meanwhile, rinse the rice until the water runs clear, then drain.

Heat 2 tablespoons of ghee or oil in a heavy-based pan on a medium
heat. Add the rice and stir until coated. Add 450ml/2 cups of the
water and bring to a boil. Stir in ½ teaspoon of salt. Turn the heat
to the lowest setting, cover and cook for 25–30 minutes, until the
water has been absorbed and the rice is tender.

Preheat the oven to 425°F. Line a large baking sheet with parchment
paper. Split the pita breads horizontally into two thin halves, then
tear or cut them into bite-sized pieces. Spread on the baking sheet
and bake for 10–12 minutes, turning them halfway through, until
golden brown and crisp.

Heat the remaining 2 tablespoons ghee or oil in a pan over medium
heat. Add the garlic and cook until lightly golden. Add the tomato
paste and cook for 2–3 minutes, stirring. Add the cumin and vinegar
and stir for a few seconds. Add the remaining 400ml/1½ cups of
water, stir until well blended, season and simmer for 15 minutes
until reduced and thickened.

To assemble: spread the baked pita on a serving platter, top with
the rice, then add the lamb and some stock. Drizzle some tomato
sauce over the top. Serve with extra stock and tomato sauce on
the side.

INTLAK ALSAIEGH'S *Kubba Haleb*

IRAQI LAMB CROQUETTES

I've worked at Al-Manaar since 2001 and have seen the power of food in creating a welcoming atmosphere. People of different nationalities are sometimes fearful of each other – sharing food helps them to relax and the bonds of friendship are made. These meat-filled croquettes are something I make whenever we have guests. We never make small quantities: we cook for large numbers and we put all the food on the table at the same time.

MAKES 30 KUBBA

375g/2 cups basmati rice, soaked in cold water for 30 minutes, then rinsed and drained

1 tbsp ground turmeric

300ml/1¼ cups water

For the filling

1 tbsp olive oil

1 small onion, finely chopped

450g/1 lb ground lamb (20% fat)

2½ tbsp *baharat* (Lebanese spice mix, see page 34)

40g/¼ cup raisins, roughly chopped

25g/3 tbsp pine nuts

2–3 tbsp freshly chopped parsley

1–2 tbsp sunflower oil

salt and pepper

NOTE If you don't want to cook all the *kubba* at once, freeze once molded and use within 1 month (defrost thoroughly before cooking).

Put the rice in a pan, add the turmeric and a generous pinch of salt. Pour in the water and stir well. Bring to a boil, reduce the heat, cover with a lid and simmer for 20–25 minutes, until the water has been absorbed. Remove the pan from the heat, keeping the lid on, and set aside for 30 minutes. Do not lift the lid.

Meanwhile, heat the oil in a large pan over medium heat and cook the onion for 5 minutes or until soft. Increase the heat, add the lamb and a little salt and pepper and cook for 5 minutes, until browned, breaking up the lamb as it cooks. Stir in the *baharat*, raisins and pine nuts, and cook for another 5 minutes until the lamb is cooked through (add up to 2 tablespoons of water if the mixture seems dry). Remove the pan from the heat, taste and adjust the seasoning and let it cool. Stir in the parsley.

Transfer the cooled rice to a food processor and pulse to form a tacky dough (leave some grains intact for texture). If the rice has dried out slightly, gradually add up to 2 tablespoons of water and briefly pulse again. When you reach the desired consistency, transfer to a bowl.

Line a baking sheet with parchment paper. Weigh out 25g/scant 1 oz rice dough. With wet hands, roll the dough into a ball then use your thumb to flatten into a disk in the palm of your hand. Place 15g/½ oz lamb filling in the center of the disk and bring the edges of the dough together to encase the lamb, gently molding it into an oval torpedo shape. Repeat with the rest of the dough and lamb filling, placing them on the lined baking sheet. Let them rest for 30 minutes.

Preheat the oven to 425°F. Brush the *kubba* with sunflower oil. Bake on the top rack for 20–25 minutes. Serve immediately.

SPICED POTATO KIBBEH

This mix of potato and bulgur wheat was always on our table back in Baghdad. Moist on the inside, crispy on the outside, it goes with just about anything. You can find the *baharat* spice mix in Middle Eastern food shops and some supermarkets, or you can make your own (see below). This makes about 4 tablespoons: enough for all the recipes in the book. It will keep for 6 months in an airtight container.

SERVES 4

500g/1 lb russet potatoes, peeled and quartered

175g/1 cup plus 1 tbsp fine bulgur wheat

2 scallions, finely chopped

¼ tsp paprika

¼ tsp *baharat* (Lebanese spice mix, see below)

¼ tsp ground cumin

25g/3 tbsp pine nuts, toasted (see page 127)

2 tbsp all-purpose flour

3 tbsp olive oil, plus extra for greasing

salt and pepper

For the baharat *spice mix*

1 tbsp ground cinnamon

1½ tsp ground cumin

1½ tsp ground coriander

1½ tsp ground allspice

1½ tsp freshly ground black pepper

1½ tsp paprika

¼ tsp grated nutmeg

¼ tsp ground cloves

⅛ tsp ground cardamom

If making your own *baharat* spice mix, simply mix all the spices until well blended. Store in an airtight container.

Put the potatoes in a pot, cover with cold water and bring to a boil. Add 1 teaspoon of salt and cook for 20–30 minutes or until tender when pierced with a knife.

Soak the bulgur wheat in cold water for 10 minutes, then drain, tip onto a piece of cheesecloth and squeeze dry.

Preheat the oven to 400°F. Brush a 23cm/9-inch shallow cake pan or fluted tart pan with olive oil.

When the potatoes are cooked, drain in a colander and place the colander back in the pan for 5 minutes. The steam from the hot pan will help dry the potatoes.

While the potatoes are still warm, press them through a ricer into a large bowl. Add the bulgur, scallions, spices, nuts and flour and mix until thoroughly combined.

Firmly press the mixture into the oiled cake pan: it should be about 2.5cm/1-inch thick. Score the top into eight portions and make a 1cm/½-inch hole in the center. Drizzle with the olive oil and bake for 30–40 minutes or until the top is golden and crisp. Let cool before serving.

AYSHA BORA'S *Vada*

POTATO FRITTERS WITH CILANTRO CHUTNEY

I work at Al-Manaar and on the day of the Grenfell disaster I helped cook for 200 people – it was the first time I'd ever cooked for anyone outside my family. My mum, who is from Mumbai, used to make these fritters for us. They're very tasty – put them on the table and they'll vanish in an instant.

MAKES 10; SERVES 4-6

1 tbsp olive oil
2.5cm/1-in piece fresh
    ginger, grated
1 green chile, seeded and
    finely chopped
¼ tsp ground turmeric
5g/¼ cup cilantro, chopped
450g/1 lb mashed potato
juice of ½ lemon
2 tsp sugar
salt
6½ cups sunflower oil

For the batter
150g/1⅔ cups chickpea flour
¼ tsp chile powder
¼ tsp asafoetida
½ tsp baking soda
1 tbsp olive oil
180ml/¾ cup water

For the cilantro chutney
75g/4 cups cilantro
3 garlic cloves, peeled
4 green chiles, seeded
60g/2½ oz *nylon sev*
    (see note)
7 tbsp water
1 tsp ground cumin
¼ tsp salt

Heat the olive oil in a large pan over medium–high heat. When hot, add the ginger, chile, turmeric and cilantro and cook for 1 minute. Add the mashed potato, lemon juice, sugar and a pinch of salt, mix well and sauté over medium heat for 3–4 minutes. Taste to check for seasoning, then transfer to a plate, spread out and let cool for 20 minutes.

Meanwhile, add the batter ingredients to a mixing bowl and whisk to form a smooth batter. Transfer to the fridge to rest until needed.

To make the chutney, put the cilantro, garlic, chiles and *sev* into a food processor and blitz until well combined, gradually adding the water until you reach the desired consistency. Stir in the cumin and salt, taste to check for seasoning and set aside.

Divide the cooled potato mix into ten equal pieces and roll them into balls. Place back on the plate and transfer to the fridge for 25 minutes to firm up before coating and frying.

In a large heavy pan, heat the sunflower oil to 350°F. Gather the potato balls and batter from the fridge. Dip three of the balls in the batter, turn to coat completely and then carefully place in the hot oil, using a metal spoon or tongs. Gently push the fritters around in the oil to get an even color and fry for 3–4 minutes. Transfer to a plate lined with paper towels and repeat with the remaining balls, in batches.

Serve hot, with the cilantro chutney.

NOTE *Nylon sev* are crisp little noodles made from chickpea flour and spices, sold in Indian stores and online.

OXANA SINITSYNA'S

STUFFED PEPPERS

This is such a good sharing dish, especially if you have vegetarian guests. Just make sure they help themselves first, because the meat-eaters will all want some as well.

SERVES 4-6

150g/5 oz feta cheese

3 garlic cloves, finely chopped

10g/½ cup fresh parsley, chopped

1 tsp freshly ground black pepper

8 romano peppers or other long, sweet peppers

4 tbsp olive oil

Preheat the oven to 400°F.

Place the feta, garlic, parsley and black pepper in a mixing bowl and mash together with the back of a fork to form a paste.

Cut the stalk ends off the peppers, then carefully remove the seeds. Stuff each pepper with the feta mixture, using a small spoon to push it down into the cavities. Brush the peppers all over with 1 tablespoon of the oil.

Transfer the stuffed peppers to a large baking dish, so they fit together quite tightly, and spoon over the remaining oil. Bake for 35–40 minutes, until soft and beginning to char.

Serve hot with fresh crusty bread.

VEGETABLE SAMOSAS

Grenfell was a real community and my neighbor Rania and I used to party with food all the time. The first time I made these samosas for her, she ate ten of them. Really! They look like a lot of work, but if you have a food processor to chop the vegetables it's very easy. Use my quick way of folding them too, to save time. Just be sure to make enough…

MAKES 12 SAMOSAS

1 potato
3 tbsp vegetable oil, plus
    extra for brushing
1 tsp mustard seeds
¼ tsp fenugreek seeds
½ tsp cumin seeds
1 onion, finely sliced
½ tsp ground turmeric
½ tsp ground cinnamon
120g/4½ oz green cabbage,
    finely sliced
1 large carrot, grated
100g/3½ oz mixed red
    and green bell peppers,
    cored, seeded and finely
    chopped
50g/½ cup frozen peas
½ tsp salt
½ tsp sugar
12 spring roll pastry wrappers,
    25 x 25cm/10 x 10 in
1 egg, lightly beaten

NOTE You can also make spring rolls with this filling. Filled samosas can be frozen for up to 8 weeks. Bake them from frozen for 20 minutes.

Boil the potato in salted water for 30 minutes or until tender. Drain and let cool, then peel and dice.

Heat the vegetable oil in a large pan over medium heat. Add the spice seeds and fry for 30 seconds, until fragrant. Add the onion and a pinch of salt and cook for about 2 minutes, until translucent. Add the turmeric and cinnamon and stir for a few seconds until the onion is coated with spices. Add the cabbage, carrot and peppers and cook over high heat for 4–5 minutes or until tender.

Add the diced potato, peas, salt and sugar and stir for a couple of minutes. Taste and adjust the seasoning. Transfer to a large plate or a tray and let cool.

Cut each wrapper in half to make two rectangle strips. Keep the wrappers covered with a clean, damp cloth to stop them from drying out. Working with one strip at a time and with a long edge facing you, fold the bottom right-hand corner of the strip to meet the top edge, forming a triangle, then fold the top right-hand corner over to meet the top left-hand corner of the strip, forming a square shape. Brush the single layer of pastry (bottom left) with some beaten egg and fold over to form a triangular pouch. Open the pouch and fill with about 3 tablespoons of the samosa filling. Brush the pointy end with beaten egg and fold over to seal the pouch. Place on a tray and keep covered while you make the rest of the samosas.

Preheat the oven to 425°F and line a baking sheet with parchment paper. Place the samosas on the baking sheet. Brush the tops with a little oil and then with some beaten egg. Bake for 10 minutes, then turn them over, brush the other side with oil and egg and bake for another 10 minutes or until golden.

FAIZA HAYANI BELLILI'S *Lham Lahlou*

ALGERIAN SWEET LAMB

In Algeria, this special dish is on the table every day during Ramadan. Although it's made with meat, it's very sweet from the dried fruits and you eat it last in the meal, like a dessert. It gives that moment of sweetness that rounds everything off.

SERVES 4-6
250g/2 cups pitted prunes
150g/¾ cup dried apricots
100g/⅔ cup dried figs, halved
25g/3 tbsp golden raisins
50g/¼ cup ghee or butter
1 onion, finely chopped
500g/1 lb lamb shoulder, trimmed and cut into 2cm/¾-in pieces
2 cinnamon sticks
1 star anise
¼ tsp salt
250ml/1 cup freshly made strong black tea
250ml/1 cup boiling water
200g/1 cup sugar
1 tsp orange blossom water
toasted sliced almonds, to serve (see page 127)

Put the dried fruits into a bowl, add boiling water to cover and set aside for 30 minutes.

Meanwhile, heat the ghee or butter in a large pan over medium heat, add the onion and cook for 10 minutes, until golden. Add the lamb, cinnamon, star anise and salt and cook for 12–15 minutes, until the lamb is well browned.

Add the tea, cover the pan and simmer for 30 minutes or until reduced and thick.

Add the boiling water, sugar and orange blossom water and stir until the sugar has dissolved. Drain the soaked dried fruits, add to the pan and stir well. Simmer, uncovered, over medium–low heat for 20 minutes, until the sauce has reduced and thickened, and the mixture is glossy.

Serve warm on small plates, garnished with toasted sliced almonds.

GREEN CHILE & AVOCADO DIP

 My life-long dream has been to have a food van; I spend any free time I have thinking up dishes, and putting ingredients together in my mind. These dips are my own invention.

SERVES 4

2 green chiles, halved
    and seeded
25g/1¼ cups cilantro leaves
3 tbsp plain yogurt
grated zest and juice of
    2 lemons
4 garlic cloves, peeled
1 ripe avocado, peeled and
    pitted
4 tbsp mayonnaise
    (optional)
salt and pepper

Put all the ingredients except the mayonnaise into a food processor and blend until smooth. Taste and adjust the seasoning if necessary. Add the mayonnaise (if you wish) and stir to combine, then transfer to a serving bowl.

MUNIRA MAHMUD'S

GREEN CHILE & TOMATO DIP

 You can enjoy this dip with just about anything – it's quite spicy, but so tasty!

SERVES 4

2 green chiles, halved
    and seeded
½ onion, finely chopped
juice of 1 lemon
2 ripe tomatoes, quartered
20g/1 cup cilantro leaves
salt and pepper

Blend all the ingredients together in a food processor. Taste and adjust the seasoning if necessary, then transfer to a serving bowl.

TZATZIKI

☼ I got this recipe from my Irish mum – but I don't know where she got it from! It's great in the summer because it's very cooling. Make it ahead of time and leave it in the fridge to let the flavors develop.

SERVES 4-6
1 cucumber, 300g/10 oz
1⅔ cups Greek yogurt
2 garlic cloves, minced
juice of ½ lemon
1 tbsp olive oil
salt and pepper

Peel the cucumber and halve lengthwise. Scoop out the seeds with a spoon, then grate the flesh. Squeeze out the water from the grated flesh, then place in a bowl. Add the yogurt, garlic, lemon juice, olive oil, and salt and pepper to taste; mix well to combine.

Chill in the fridge for 30 minutes before serving alongside pita bread or grilled lamb.

HUMMUS

✳ I've always made my own hummus: it's so easy if you have a food processor. One day a Turkish friend told me to add fresh cilantro – I've never looked back! *Pictured on page 49.*

SERVES 4
4 tbsp tahini
juice of 1 lemon
2 garlic cloves, minced
1 (425g/15.5 oz) can
    chickpeas, drained
3 tbsp olive oil, plus extra
    to drizzle
4½ tbsp water
10g/½ cup cilantro, chopped
pinch of paprika
salt and pepper

Put the tahini and lemon juice in a food processor and blitz for about 30 seconds until combined. Add the garlic, chickpeas and olive oil and blitz until combined and thick. Gradually add the water until you reach the desired consistency. Season to taste, then stir in most of the chopped cilantro.

Spoon into a serving bowl and top with a drizzle of olive oil, a pinch of paprika and the remaining cilantro.

CLAREN BILAL'S

SPICY PEANUT DIP

✳✳✳
✳✳✳   I wanted to cook something really typical from Uganda, where we often use ground nuts
to make a peanut butter that we call *nino*. But our cuisine in the north of the country is quite spicy and I didn't think all the other ladies at the Hubb Kitchen would like it – so I made it into a dip to have on the side. Turns out it goes with just about everything!

SERVES 4-6

1 tbsp olive oil
1 onion, finely chopped
2 garlic cloves, crushed
1 tsp grated fresh ginger
1 red chile, finely chopped
1½ tsp ground coriander
1½ tsp ground cumin
½ tsp paprika
½ tsp ground cardamom
1 tbsp tomato paste
400ml/1⅔ cups water
100g/6 tbsp peanut butter
salt and cayenne pepper

Heat the oil in a pan over medium heat and cook the onion for 10 minutes, until lightly browned. Add the garlic, ginger and chile and cook for a couple of minutes, stirring all the time. Add all the spices and cook for 30 seconds, until fragrant, then add the tomato paste and the water and simmer for 5 minutes.

Finally, add the peanut butter and stir until the mixture is smooth. Simmer for 5 minutes. The sauce should be thick but pourable. Add a little more water if needed.

Taste and add salt and a pinch of cayenne pepper if needed. Serve as a dip with naan bread or as a sauce over roasted sweet potatoes or rice.

BABA GANOUSH

You'll find versions of this dip all over the Middle East. My mum taught me this recipe when I was 15 years old and I've made it ever since. It has a lovely smoky flavor and – once the eggplant is cooked – takes no time at all. *Pictured opposite (below), with Hummus (top; see page 46).*

SERVES 4

1 large or 2 medium
    eggplants, about
    550g/1¼ lb
3 tbsp tahini
1 garlic clove, finely chopped
1 tbsp white wine vinegar
pinch of cayenne pepper,
    plus extra to garnish
1 tbsp freshly chopped
    parsley
salt

Preheat the oven to 450°F. Place the eggplant in a baking dish and roast for 40–45 minutes, or until well charred and soft. Set aside to cool.

When the eggplant is cool enough to handle, peel off the skin and place the flesh in a bowl. Using a fork, beat the eggplant until it forms a smooth puree.

Spoon the tahini into a separate bowl. Dilute with 1 tablespoon of warm water; at first it will thicken. Add another tablespoon of water and mix until the tahini becomes creamy again. Add the garlic, vinegar and eggplant puree and mix until well blended. Season with salt and cayenne pepper, then gently mix in the parsley.

Spoon into a serving bowl and sprinkle with a little more cayenne pepper to serve.

LUNCHES
AND DINNERS

INTLAK ALSAIEGH'S *Tepsi Baytinijan*

BEEF & EGGPLANT CASSEROLE

Tepsi translates as "casserole" and this is a traditional Persian dish of meatballs in tomato sauce with eggplant. It's quite rich. You could make it with less oil, I suppose, but then it wouldn't be so traditional – or taste so good.

SERVES 4-6

350g/¾ pound ground beef
4 large garlic cloves, minced
¾ tsp curry powder
2 eggplants, about
    700g/1½ lb, cut into
    1.5cm/½-in slices
120ml/½ cup olive oil
2 large potatoes, about
    500g/1 lb, peeled and cut
    into 1.5cm/½-in slices
1 large onion, peeled and cut
    into 1cm/½-in slices
1 large green pepper, cored,
    seeded and sliced
350ml/1½ cups water
4 tbsp tomato paste
1½ tbsp tamarind paste
1½ tbsp sugar
3 ripe tomatoes, about
    280g/10 oz, cut into
    1cm/½-in slices
salt and white pepper

Preheat the oven to 400°F.

Place the beef and half of the crushed garlic in a bowl. Add the curry powder and mix by hand until well combined. Divide the mixture into 12 equal pieces and roll into balls. Set aside.

Heat a large non-stick pan over medium–high heat. Brush both sides of the eggplant slices with olive oil and cook in batches for 4–5 minutes on each side, until golden. Set aside.

Brush the potato slices with oil and cook in the same pan for about 6 minutes on each side until golden but not completely cooked through. Set aside.

In the same pan, cook the onion slices and green pepper in about 2 tablespoons of the oil for about 5 minutes, until just golden. Add the remaining garlic and cook for 1 more minute. Set aside.

Finally, cook the meatballs over high heat for 2–3 minutes until well browned but not cooked through.

In a measuring cup, mix the water with the tomato paste, tamarind paste and sugar until well blended.

Arrange half of the eggplant, potato, onion, pepper, tomatoes and meatballs in a 30cm/12-inch round baking dish, overlapping them. Season well with salt and pepper, then pour half of the tomato sauce over the top. Repeat with the rest of the vegetables and meatballs. Season well again and pour the remaining sauce on top.

Cover with foil and lid and bake for 30 minutes, then uncover and bake for another 20 minutes. Serve with basmati rice or bread to mop up the sauce.

SPICED LAMB PILAO

Many cultures have their own version of this dish and mine has Asian and Arab influences. But the thing to know about pilao is that you have to make it your own. It's trial and error really. Just play around, adding your favorite spices – this recipe is how my family likes it, so you can use it as your starting point.

SERVES 4-6

4 tbsp sunflower oil

2 large onions, finely
   chopped

900g/2 lb boneless lamb
   shoulder, cut into chunks

2 tbsp grated fresh ginger

2 tbsp minced garlic

2 tbsp cumin seeds

8 cardamom pods, crushed

6 cloves

4 cinnamon sticks

550ml/2⅓ cups water

350g/1¾ cups basmati rice

salt and pepper

For the minted yogurt

150g/⅔ cup plain yogurt

small handful of mint leaves,
   sliced

Heat 2 tablespoons of the oil in a large heavy pan over medium heat. Add the onions and cook for 10 minutes until soft and golden.

Remove the onions from the pan and set aside. Add the remaining oil, then cook the lamb, in batches, until browned. Return all the browned lamb to the pan along with the cooked onions, ginger, garlic, cumin seeds, cardamom pods, cloves, cinnamon sticks and a pinch of salt and pepper. Mix well to combine. Add 400ml/1⅔ cups of the water and bring to a boil. Reduce the heat to a gentle simmer, cover with a lid and cook over low heat for 3 hours, stirring occasionally and adding extra water if it starts to dry out.

Once the lamb is very tender, add the rice and the remaining 150ml/⅔ cup water, stir and bring to a boil. Reduce the heat, cover with a tight-fitting lid and cook for 15 minutes without removing the lid. Remove the pan from the heat, keeping the lid firmly on, and set aside for 15 minutes.

Meanwhile, combine the yogurt with the mint leaves.

Remove the lid and use a large fork to fluff up the rice. Taste and adjust the seasoning and serve with the minted yogurt alongside.

PERSIAN LAMB & HERB STEW

My family is originally from Pakistan and my husband is from Iran. When I looked into it, I found connections between the Pakistani and Persian cultures going way back, which I try to bring into my recipes. This dish is my husband's favorite, so naturally it was the first one I learned to cook after we got married.

SERVES 4

5 tbsp vegetable oil

1 onion, finely chopped

4 garlic cloves, finely chopped

1 tsp ground turmeric

500g/1 lb boneless lamb shoulder, cut into 2cm/¾-in cubes

600ml/2½ cups water

4 Persian dried limes (available in Middle Eastern shops or online), each pierced with a knife

100g/5 cups fresh flat-leaf parsley

75g/3½ cups cilantro

75g/3½ cups fresh chives

50g/1 cup fresh fenugreek leaves (often sold as *methi*; substitute 1 tbsp dried fenugreek leaves if you can't find it fresh)

1 tsp tomato paste

1 (400g/14.5 oz) can red kidney beans, drained and rinsed

salt and pepper

Heat 2 tablespoons of the oil in a large pan and cook the onion and garlic over medium–high heat for 10 minutes, until golden. Add the turmeric and stir for 30 seconds until the onions are well coated. Add the meat, season with salt and pepper and cook for about 10 minutes, until browned.

Add the water and the dried limes. Bring to a boil and skim off any foam on the surface. Lower the heat, cover and simmer for 1½ hours.

While the meat is cooking, wash, dry and chop the herbs.

Heat the remaining 3 tablespoons oil in a large pan and stir-fry the herbs for 5–7 minutes, until wilted. Add the herbs and tomato paste to the meat and simmer for 30 minutes. Then add the beans and simmer for a final 30 minutes.

Taste and adjust the seasoning and remove the dried limes. Serve with plain white rice and Shirazi Salad (see page 95).

IRAQI DOLMA

I wasn't taught to cook; it was just what we did at home in Baghdad with my mother and mother-in-law. You knew you'd got it right when guests asked for recipes. This is a colorful dish – color is important in Iraqi cooking. The pomegranate molasses and *baharat* spice (see page 34) are what give it the Persian flavor.

SERVES 4-6

4 onions, peeled

280g/1½ cups basmati rice, rinsed and soaked in cold water for 30 minutes, then drained

280g/⅔ lb ground lamb

3 ripe tomatoes, chopped

2 garlic cloves, finely chopped

3 tbsp tamarind paste

3 tbsp pomegranate molasses

6 tbsp tomato paste

8 tbsp olive oil

2 tsp *baharat* (Lebanese spice mix, see page 34)

2 tsp salt

4 long green peppers or romano peppers, cored and seeded

20 large grape leaves (preserved in brine), soaked in boiling water for 20 minutes, then drained and refreshed under cold water

600ml/2½ cups water

Make an incision in the onions from top to bottom on one side, cutting halfway through, stopping at the core. Bring a pan of water to a boil, add the onions and simmer for 12 minutes. Drain and rinse under cold water. When cool, separate each onion to make two or three shells (each shell will have two layers) and a small core. You need eight shells in total. Chop the onion cores and set aside.

Place the rice in a bowl. Add the lamb, chopped onion, tomatoes, garlic, 1½ tablespoons of the tamarind paste, 1½ tablespoons of the pomegranate molasses, 3 tablespoons of the tomato paste, 4 tablespoons of the olive oil, the spice mix and 1½ teaspoons of salt. Mix delicately with your hands until well blended, taking care not to break the rice too much.

Make an incision in the peppers from top to bottom and fill with some of the rice mixture; don't pack too tightly, as the rice expands as it cooks. Fill the onion shells likewise.

Place 1 heaping tablespoon of rice mixture in the center of each grape leaf, near the stem. Fold the stem end over the filling, fold in both sides and roll up loosely to allow space for the rice to expand.

Snugly fit the stuffed vegetables in a large pan with a tight-fitting lid. Mix the remaining tamarind paste, pomegranate molasses, tomato paste, salt and olive oil with the water, then pour over the dolma. Invert a large plate on top to hold everything in place. Cover, bring to a boil, then simmer over low heat for 45 minutes to 1 hour, or until the rice is cooked and most of the liquid has been absorbed.

Remove the plate, place a large serving platter over the pan and carefully flip the contents onto the platter. (*Pictured overleaf*)

GREEN RICE

I have a master's degree in chemistry, but when I came to Britain from Iraq it wasn't easy to combine that with family life, so now the kitchen is my laboratory. With the mixing, pouring and measuring I feel like I am back in my old world. This is a version of a traditional dish, which I made up. It's a good centerpiece because the color is so striking.

SERVES 4

500g/1 lb lamb neck fillet or boneless lamb shoulder, cut into 3cm/1 in cubes
1 liter/1 quart chicken stock (made with 2 stock cubes)
300g/1½ cups basmati rice
250g/1½ cups frozen fava beans
4 tbsp sunflower oil
2 garlic cloves, minced
40g/2 cups fresh dill, finely chopped
2 tbsp dried dill

For the Cucumber, Dill & Yogurt Sauce
1 cucumber, coarsely grated
500g/2 cups plain full-fat yogurt
1 tsp dried dill
1 tbsp olive oil
salt and pepper

Place the lamb and stock in a large pan and bring to a boil. Skim off the foam on the surface, reduce the heat to medium–low and gently simmer for 1 hour (or 1½ hours if you are using lamb shoulder), until cooked through.

Rinse the rice and let soak for 30 minutes. Blanch the fava beans in a pot of boiling water for 2–3 minutes, drain and refresh under cold water. Remove the outer skins.

When the lamb is cooked, strain and reserve the stock. Heat half of the oil in a heavy pan and cook the garlic until it just starts to color. Add the lamb and cook for 5–6 minutes until evenly browned, stirring all the time. Add the fava beans and half of the fresh and dried dill and cook for 2 minutes. Set aside and keep warm.

In the same pan, heat the remaining oil over medium–low heat. Drain the rice and add to the pan, stirring until all the grains are coated with oil. Add 500ml/2 cups of the reserved stock, bring to a simmer, cover tightly, then turn the heat to the lowest setting and cook for 30 minutes.

Meanwhile, make the yogurt sauce. Mix the grated cucumber and yogurt in a bowl. Season with salt and pepper to taste. Sprinkle with the dried dill and drizzle with olive oil.

When the rice is ready, stir it with a fork to fluff it. Add the rest of the fresh and dried dill, the reserved meat and fava beans and stir gently. Add a little of the reserved stock if you need extra moisture and cook over low heat for about 8 minutes. Serve immediately, with cucumber, dill and yogurt sauce.

PERSIAN CHICKEN WITH BARBERRY RICE

This dish is a favorite of mine and always seems to please guests at the dinner table. The jeweled rice gives it a sweet, tangy, mouthwatering taste and, although it takes a bit of time, it's pretty easy to make. It's worth the time because the end result is so spectacular.

SERVES 4-6

For the chicken

2 small ice cubes

generous pinch of saffron
   threads, ground to
   a powder

2 tbsp butter

8 bone-in skinless chicken
   thighs (or buy with skin
   on, pull off the skin
   and discard)

2 onions, peeled:
   1 quartered,
   1 thinly sliced

1 tsp ground turmeric

1 tsp salt

1 tsp freshly ground
   black pepper

700ml/3 cups water

2 tbsp ghee or vegetable oil

2 tbsp tomato paste

2 tbsp freshly squeezed
   lemon juice

1 tbsp dried barberries,
   rinsed

Continued overleaf

For the chicken: Place the ice cubes in a small bowl, sprinkle the saffron over the top and set aside. As the ice melts, the saffron will slowly release its bright orange color and pungent flavor.

Melt the butter in a large pot over medium heat and cook the chicken pieces for 5 minutes on each side, until lightly golden. Add the onion quarters, sprinkle with the turmeric, salt and pepper and cover with water. Bring to a boil and skim off any foam on the surface. Lower the heat, cover and simmer for 15 minutes. Turn the chicken and simmer, covered, for another 15 minutes.

Meanwhile, cook the sliced onion in the ghee or vegetable oil for 10–15 minutes, until golden brown. Add the tomato paste and stir for a minute to coat the onion. Set aside.

Remove about half of the stock and the onion quarters from the chicken pan. Reserve the stock for later (save the onions for a soup or a stew).

Pour the saffron water over the chicken. Add the cooked sliced onion, the lemon juice and barberries and stir well. Cover and simmer for 15 minutes.

(This is a good point to start making the barberry rice; see overleaf.)

Turn the chicken thighs again and simmer, covered, for a final 15 minutes. The sauce should be reduced and glossy. If the sauce is too thin, remove the chicken and boil to reduce until thick; if it is too thick, add some of the reserved stock. Keep warm while you finish the rice.

Continued overleaf

For the barberry rice

2 liters/2 quarts water

400g/2 cups basmati rice

½ tsp ground cinnamon

½ tsp dried crushed edible
    rose petals

¼ tsp ground cumin

⅛ tsp ground cardamom

1 tbsp salt

5 tbsp ghee or vegetable oil

1 onion, finely chopped

25g/3 tbsp dried barberries,
    rinsed and soaked for
    15 minutes

almonds and/or pistachios,
    to garnish

For the barberry rice: In a large heavy pan (with a tight-fitting lid), bring the water to a boil.

Put the rice in a bowl and rinse several times under running water, stirring gently with your fingers. When the water is clear, drain the rice.

Mix the cinnamon, rose petals, cumin and cardamom until well blended. Set aside.

Add the salt to the boiling water, then add the rice. Let the water come back to a boil, stir the rice and cook, uncovered, for about 7 minutes. It should be soft on the outside and slightly hard inside.

Drain the rice. Return the pan to the heat and add 3 tablespoons of ghee or vegetable oil. Spoon half of the rice into the pan, then sprinkle with half of the spices. Spoon the remaining rice on top and sprinkle with the remaining spices. Poke the handle of the spoon into the rice, making five holes to let the steam escape. Wrap the lid in a clean dish towel and place on top of the pan. Turn the heat to low and cook for 30 minutes.

For the rice garnish, heat the remaining 2 tablespoons of ghee or vegetable oil in a small pan over medium heat and cook the onion for 10 minutes, until golden. Drain the barberries and squeeze out the excess water. Add them to the onion and stir for 30 seconds, taking care as the barberries tend to burn easily.

When ready to serve, stir the rice gently with a fork to mix the spices evenly and spoon onto a serving plate. Garnish with the onion and barberry mixture and sprinkle chopped almonds and/or pistachios over the top. Serve with the chicken.

ALGERIAN COUSCOUS

I used to run my own translation agency in Algeria. When I moved to London I very much missed my work and was initially quite lonely. So, while my children napped, I cooked. Cooking became an important connection to home for me. It eventually led me here to the Community Kitchen, where I made great friends. This is a traditional Algerian dish (we use any veg we have on hand), including the proper way to cook couscous.

SERVES 4

3 tbsp olive oil

1 onion, chopped

1 large garlic clove, minced

1 chicken, about 1.6kg/3½ lb, cut into 8 pieces

1 heaping tsp ras-el-hanout spice mix

1 large carrot, peeled and cut into 4 chunks

1 large yellow or red potato, peeled and quartered

1 small rutabaga, peeled and cut into 3cm/1¼-in chunks

1 large celery stick, cut into 4

800ml/3½ cups water

2 tsp salt

½ tsp ground black pepper

1 mild green chile

1 large zucchini, cut into 4

1 large parsnip, peeled, quartered, core removed

200g/7 oz canned chopped tomatoes

100g/4 oz canned chickpeas, rinsed

¼ tsp dried mint

300g/2 cups couscous

2 tbsp ghee or butter, melted

Heat the oil in a large pan, add the onion, garlic and chicken and cook over medium–high heat for 6–7 minutes until golden. Add the ras-el-hanout and stir until the ingredients are well coated with spice. Transfer to a couscous pot or a heavy pot with a lid. Add the carrot, potato, rutabaga, celery and water and bring to a boil. Skim off the foam, add 1½ teaspoons of salt, the black pepper and the whole green chile. Lower the heat, cover and simmer for 40 minutes.

Add the zucchini, parsnip, tomatoes, chickpeas, mint and a little more water if needed. Simmer, covered, for 30 minutes.

Spread the couscous in a large shallow dish. Dissolve ½ teaspoon of salt in 120ml/½ cup of warm water. Sprinkle the salted water over the grains and mix with your hands until all the grains are wet. Set aside for 5 minutes. Break up the couscous with your fingers, rolling some of it between your palms to separate and aerate the grains.

If you are using a couscous pot, line the top with cheesecloth, add the couscous and cover with the lid. Alternatively, set a fine-mesh sieve over a pot of boiling water, add the couscous to the sieve and cover tightly with foil to prevent the steam escaping. Steam the couscous for 12 minutes.

Return the couscous to the dish and, when cool enough to handle, mix the couscous by hand, as before, to separate and aerate the grains. Repeat the steaming and mixing two more times. When the couscous is ready, drizzle the ghee or butter over the top and mix delicately, using two forks, until all the ghee is incorporated.

Spoon the couscous onto serving plates. Add some chicken and vegetables and ladle sauce on top. Serve the extra sauce on the side.

AYSHA BORA'S *Kuku Paka*

COCONUT CHICKEN CURRY

✱✱✱ When I was growing up I hated cooking. My family is from India and preparing big meals
✱✱✱ for the extended family was part of our culture, but I used to beg for any job other than
cooking. Then I got married and moved to Africa and suddenly everything changed – I began
calling my mother and asking her for recipes. She told me: "Cooking for someone you love is
what makes you a good cook." This curry is a particular favorite of my family in Tanzania.

SERVES 4

1 large chicken, cut into
    8 pieces, excess skin
    trimmed away
1 large ripe tomato,
    roughly chopped
1 onion, peeled and
    quartered
2cm/¾-in piece fresh ginger,
    peeled
4 garlic cloves, peeled
6 serrano chiles, stemmed
    and seeded (use less if
    you prefer milder curries)
2 tsp ground cumin
1 tsp ground coriander
1 tsp ground turmeric
2 tbsp coconut oil
2 (400ml/14.5 oz) cans
    coconut milk
3 eggs, hard-boiled, peeled
    and halved
juice of ½ lemon
salt and pepper
10g/½ cup cilantro,
    chopped, to garnish
rice, chapati or flatbread,
    to serve

Score each piece of chicken in two or three places, slicing about 1cm/½ inch into the meat.

Put the tomato, onion, ginger, garlic, chiles, cumin, coriander, turmeric and some salt and pepper into a food processor and blend to a rough paste. Rub one third of the paste all over the chicken, into the cuts and under the skin; reserve the rest of the paste. Refrigerate the chicken for at least 1 hour, or up to 5 hours.

Preheat the broiler to the highest setting, and line a large baking sheet with foil.

In a large pan, heat the coconut oil over medium heat; add the reserved paste and cook, stirring occasionally, for 20 minutes or until all of the moisture evaporates. Increase the heat slightly and cook for 3–5 minutes until the paste is thick and dark. Add the coconut milk and simmer for 25–30 minutes until the sauce is thick.

Meanwhile, put the marinated chicken, skin side up, on the prepared baking sheet and broil for 15 minutes, until well colored and charred, then turn the chicken over and broil for another 5 minutes to make sure it is cooked through.

Stir the chicken and any juices into the curry pan, bring to a simmer, cover and cook for 5 minutes until the flavors have combined. Taste and adjust the seasoning if necessary. Add the boiled eggs and a squeeze of lemon juice, or more to taste. Sprinkle with fresh cilantro and serve with rice, chapati or flatbread.

AMAAL ABD ELRASOUL'S

CHICKEN & MUSHROOM CREAM SOUP

I live in Cairo, but came over after the Grenfell fire to help my sister-in-law Munira. I got this recipe from a neighbor back home. It is very special – shredded chicken in a creamy base scented with cardamom, cinnamon and ginger – so naturally I made it for the women in the Kitchen. I guarantee you haven't had chicken soup like this before.

SERVES 4

4 tbsp butter

2 onions, chopped

2 garlic cloves, thinly sliced

5 cardamom pods,
   lightly crushed

2 cloves

2 bay leaves

½ tsp ground ginger

¼ tsp ground allspice

pinch of ground cinnamon

½ chicken, about 650g/1½ lb

1 liter/1 quart water

3 tbsp all-purpose flour

150ml/⅔ cup heavy cream

250g/9 oz mushrooms,
   sliced

fresh flat-leaf parsley,
   to garnish

Melt 1 tablespoon butter in a large heavy pot over medium-low heat. Add the onions and cook for 5 minutes, until soft.

Add the garlic and spices and cook for 1 minute, until fragrant. Add the chicken, skin side down, and the water. Bring to a simmer, skim off the foam on the surface and cook for 35 minutes. Turn off the heat and let cool for about 1 hour.

When the chicken is cool enough to handle, strain the stock and reserve. Peel off and discard the chicken skin. Shred the chicken into bite-size pieces and set aside.

Melt 2 tablespoons of the butter in the pot used for the stock. Stir in the flour and cook for 1 minute, until the paste is lightly golden. Whisk in the reserved stock and the cream and bring to a simmer.

Meanwhile, melt the remaining 1 tablespoon butter in a pan over medium heat and stir-fry the mushrooms for 5 minutes, until lightly golden and the liquid has evaporated.

Add the mushrooms and shredded chicken to the soup and simmer for 10–15 minutes. Serve garnished with parsley.

JEERA CHICKEN

I was born and raised in West London but am ethnically Indian. When I was growing up, cooking was one of the ways I bonded with my mother – Mama Jay. My goal was always to make a dish so that my father and brothers assumed she had made it. This is one of her favorites. Cooked in plenty of yogurt with aromatic cumin, the curry is quick and easy to prepare and makes a delicious supper for the whole family.

SERVES 4

2 tbsp cumin seeds

2 tbsp sunflower oil

2 red onions, thinly sliced

3cm/1¼-in piece fresh
    ginger, peeled and grated

40g/1½ oz green chiles,
    seeded and sliced

2 tsp ground turmeric

1 tsp sea salt

8 bone-in skinless chicken
    thighs (or buy with skin
    on, pull off the skin
    and discard)

300–500g/1–2 cups
    plain yogurt, at room
    temperature

1½ tbsp garam masala

juice of ½ lemon

15g/¾ cup cilantro, chopped

salt and pepper

rice and/or pitas or
    flatbread, to serve

Heat a large pan over medium-low heat, add the cumin seeds and gently toast until fragrant, then transfer to a bowl and set aside. Add the oil to the pan and when it is hot, add the onions and let them gently sizzle for 10 minutes until soft and golden.

Add the toasted cumin seeds, ginger and chiles to the pan and cook for 1 minute, then add the turmeric and salt and stir to combine. Increase the heat slightly, add the chicken, and cook for about 5 minutes, then reduce the heat slightly and add 300g/1 cup yogurt to the pan, adding more as necessary to ensure the chicken is submerged in the sauce. Gently simmer, stirring often, for 30–35 minutes until the chicken is cooked through; the yogurt will split at first, but will come back together and form a creamy sauce.

Add the garam masala, lemon juice and cilantro and stir to combine. Taste and adjust the seasoning and serve immediately, with rice, pitas or flatbread.

BAKED FISH WITH TAHINI & POMEGRANATE

This is a recipe from my Algerian Dad – and it's so easy I'm almost embarrassed to call it a recipe! It works well with all kinds of fish, even salmon, and it's a great way of using up any tahini you have left over after you've made hummus.

SERVES 4

4 skinless boneless fillets of
    cod or other fish, about
    150g/5 oz each
1 tbsp olive oil
salt and pepper
4 tbsp tahini
juice of 1 lemon
1 garlic clove, minced
2–4 tbsp warm water
10g/½ cup fresh flat-leaf
    parsley, roughly torn
50g/⅓ cup fresh
    pomegranate seeds
50g/⅓ cup pine nuts, toasted
    (see page 127)

Preheat the oven to 400°F. Place the fish in a baking dish and drizzle with the oil, and season with salt and pepper, then cook for 10–12 minutes, depending on the thickness of your fish.

In a bowl, mix the tahini, lemon juice, garlic, and some salt and pepper. Gradually add the warm water until you reach the consistency of plain yogurt.

In another bowl, mix the parsley, pomegranate seeds and pine nuts. This is your garnish.

When the fish is done, pour the tahini sauce over it and sprinkle the garnish on top.

TUNA, OLIVE & SUN-DRIED TOMATO CAKE

This is so easy and quick – it has become my emergency dish! I keep all the simple pantry ingredients on hand so I can make it any time. You can serve it hot or cold and it's perfect for picnics.

SERVES 4-6

150g/1 heaping cup all-purpose flour

1 tsp baking powder

1 tsp ground turmeric

1 tsp ground cumin

3 eggs

2 (140g/5 oz) cans tuna in oil

100g/1 cup pitted mixed olives, roughly chopped

40g/¾ cup sun-dried tomatoes in oil, drained and chopped

100g/1⅓ cups grated Cheddar cheese

Preheat the oven to 400°F. Line a 21 × 11cm/8½ × 4½-inch loaf pan with parchment paper.

Place the flour, baking powder and spices in a large bowl and whisk until well blended.

Make a hollow in the center and crack in the eggs. Start mixing from the center, gradually combining the flour with the eggs until just blended. Add the tuna and its oil, the olives, sun-dried tomatoes and cheese and gently fold together with a spatula.

Pour the mixture into the prepared pan and spread evenly. Bake for 35–40 minutes, until lightly golden on top and springy to the touch. Leave to cool in the pan for 5–10 minutes before turning out. Serve hot or cold, sliced.

EGGPLANT MASALA

It was 1976 and our mother was teaching me and my teenage sisters to cook – passing on her recipes. I was the best at making eggplant masala, so she allowed me to call it my signature dish – I've made it ever since. Back home in Uganda, I run a restaurant where I serve this along with other local dishes. When I'm in London helping my daughter Munira with my grandchildren, I make it for them and for the women at the Community Kitchen.

SERVES 4

4 tbsp sunflower oil

2 large eggplants, chopped
    into 4cm/1½-in cubes

350g/12 oz new potatoes,
    halved

2 tsp cumin seeds

1 tsp mustard seeds

1 tsp fenugreek seeds

1 large onion,
    finely chopped

3 dried curry leaves

3 tbsp tomato paste

1 tbsp minced garlic

1 tbsp grated fresh ginger

1 tsp ground turmeric

4 ripe tomatoes,
    finely chopped

200ml/¾ cup water

3 tbsp freshly chopped
    cilantro

For the rice

600ml/2½ cups water

pinch of salt

300g/1½ cups basmati rice

Heat 2 tablespoons of the oil in a large pan over high heat. Add the eggplant and cook, stirring often, for 10 minutes or until well browned. Tip the eggplant into a large bowl and set aside. Reduce the heat to medium–high and add 1 tablespoon of oil to the pan. Add the potatoes and cook, stirring often, for 10 minutes or until golden brown. Transfer the potatoes to the bowl with the eggplant and set aside.

Heat a large pan over medium–high heat, add the cumin, mustard and fenugreek seeds and toast until fragrant, 2–3 minutes. Then add 1 tablespoon of oil and when it is hot, add the onion and curry leaves and cook for 10 minutes until soft and golden.

Add the tomato paste and cook for 2 minutes, then add the garlic, ginger, turmeric and tomatoes. Cook for about 5 minutes, until the tomato juice has evaporated and the mixture is starting to dry up in the pan.

Meanwhile, prepare the rice. Put the 600ml/2½ cups water and salt in a pot and bring to a boil. Add the rice, reduce the heat slightly, cover and boil for 10 minutes. Remove the pot from the heat, keeping the lid firmly on, and set aside for 10 minutes.

Add the eggplants and potatoes to the curry pan, along with the 200ml/¾ cup water. Bring to a boil, then reduce the heat to a simmer, cover and cook for 15 minutes, stirring occasionally. Remove the lid and simmer for 5–10 minutes or until the vegetables are tender. Stir in half the chopped cilantro.

Remove the lid from the rice and fluff up with a fork. Serve alongside the curry, sprinkled with the remaining cilantro.

ETHIOPIAN SPICY RED LENTILS & GREENS WITH TOMATO SALAD

Grenfell was such a great community, so it's really nice to come along to the Hubb Kitchen and be back among the people who were your neighbors; it's a real social gathering. My recipes are from Ethiopia, where I lived until I was 12. They are vegan, although you really don't miss the meat. My family isn't vegetarian, but we do like to have some meat-free meals. And if you are cooking for a crowd with many different backgrounds, as we are here, then it's good to have something everyone can eat.

Ethiopian meals are traditionally served on a large spongy flatbread called *injera*. It's tricky to make, but you can source it online (try injeraforyou.com) or at your local Ethiopian restaurant. Stews and salads are heaped directly onto the *injera*, which you tear with your fingers and use to scoop up each flavorful mouthful. Rice or bread are perfectly fine accompaniments too.

SERVES 4

For the berbere *spice mix*
2 tbsp paprika
2 tsp ground coriander
1 tsp cayenne pepper
½ tsp ground black pepper
½ tsp ground fenugreek
½ tsp ground allspice
½ tsp ground ginger
½ tsp ground cinnamon
¼ tsp ground cardamom
¼ tsp ground cloves
¼ tsp ground nutmeg
1 tsp salt

For the misir wot *(lentils)*
¼ cup vegetable oil
1½ onions, about 175g/6 oz,
 finely chopped

For the bebere *spice mix:* Mix all the spices until they are well blended. This makes more than you need for this recipe. It will keep for up to 6 months in an airtight container.

For the misir wot *(lentils):* Heat the oil in a heavy pot over medium heat and cook the onions for 5 minutes, until soft.

Add the ginger and garlic and cook for 5 minutes, until lightly brown. Add the *berbere* spice mix and cook for 1 minute, until fragrant. Add the tomato paste and cook for 1 minute, stirring until the onions are well coated.

Add the lentils and water and simmer for 25–40 minutes (depending on the brand of lentil you use), until all the water has been absorbed and the lentils are soft. Taste and adjust the seasoning.

While the lentils are cooking, you can prepare the *Gomen Wot* and Tomato Salad.

Continued overleaf

Continued overleaf

1 tbsp grated fresh ginger
3 garlic cloves, minced
1 tbsp *berbere* spice mix
   (see page 83)
3 tbsp tomato paste
200g/1 cup red lentils,
   rinsed
600ml/2½ cups water
salt

For the gomen wot *(greens)*
¼ cup vegetable oil
1 onion, very finely chopped
2 tbsp grated fresh ginger
6 garlic cloves, minced
½ tsp ground turmeric
500g/1 lb frozen whole leaf
   spinach
salt and pepper

For the tomato salad
3 ripe tomatoes, chopped
½ red onion, finely chopped
1 jalapeño pepper, seeded
   and finely chopped
juice of ½ lemon
2 tbsp rice vinegar
½ tsp salt
⅛ tsp ground black pepper
1 tsp sugar, or to taste
2 tbsp olive oil

injera, rice or bread, to serve

For the gomen wot *(greens):* Heat the oil in a pan over medium heat and cook the onion for 5 minutes, until soft. Add the ginger and garlic and cook for 5 minutes, stirring constantly, until lightly golden. Add the turmeric and cook for 30 seconds, stirring to coat the onion. Add the frozen spinach, cover and cook for 15–20 minutes, or until the spinach is fully cooked. Season with salt and pepper to taste.

For the tomato salad: Combine the tomatoes, onion and jalapeño in a bowl.

Place the lemon juice, vinegar, salt, pepper and sugar in a separate bowl and stir until the salt and sugar have dissolved. Whisk in the oil until well blended. Pour the dressing over the tomatoes and let rest for 10 minutes.

To finish: Serve the *misir wot*, *gomen wot* and salad to the table in separate bowls, accompanied by *injera*, pita or rice.

LEBANESE VEGETABLE LASAGNE

My mother was Irish, my father Algerian; I was raised in France and went to school in Switzerland, so I had a real melting pot of influences, but I definitely got my love of cooking from my father's side. In Middle Eastern culture, cooking is a show of love – and that's what we do here at the Kitchen. This vegetarian lasagne is something I developed for my kids to get them to eat more veggies. They even prefer it to the meat version.

SERVES 4

5 tbsp olive oil, plus extra
   for greasing
1 eggplant, cut into
   1.5cm/¾-in chunks
2 red peppers, cored,
   de-seeded and cut into
   1.5cm/¾-in chunks
1 zucchini, cut into
   1.5cm/¾-in chunks
1 red onion, cut into
   1.5cm/¾-in chunks
2 large ripe tomatoes,
   chopped
2 tbsp ground coriander
½ tsp crushed red pepper
   flakes, or to taste
100g/5 cups fresh spinach
10 dried lasagne sheets
350g/1½ cups plain yogurt
2 eggs
3 tbsp tahini
200g/7 oz feta cheese,
   crumbled
200g/7 oz mozzarella,
   finely chopped
salt and pepper
lemon wedges, to serve

Preheat the oven to 400°F. Grease a 20 x 30 x 5cm/9 x 13 x 2½ inches baking dish.

Heat 2 tablespoons of the oil in a large pan over medium–high heat and cook the eggplant for 10–12 minutes, until soft and golden. Season with salt and pepper and set aside.

Add 1 tablespoon of oil to the pan and cook the peppers and zucchini for 7–8 minutes, until soft and lightly brown. Season and set aside.

Add the remaining 2 tablespoons of oil to the pan and cook the onion for 5 minutes, until soft and lightly caramelized. Add the tomatoes and cook for 2 minutes, until just soft but still holding their shape. Season, add the coriander and red pepper flakes and cook until fragrant. Add the reserved eggplant, peppers and zucchini, stir to combine, then set aside.

Cook the spinach in 2 tablespoons of boiling water for 30 seconds, until just wilted. Drain and, when cool enough to handle, squeeze dry. Add to the vegetable mixture.

Drop the lasagne sheets into a pot of simmering water, in batches, for about 4–5 minutes, until pliable but not fully cooked.

In a bowl, whisk together the yogurt, eggs and tahini. Season well.

Layer a third of the vegetables in the baking dish. Top with three lasagne sheets. Spread a third of the yogurt mixture on top, then scatter over a third of both the feta and mozzarella. Repeat the layers twice, using four lasagne sheets for the final layer. Season well, then place the dish on a baking sheet. Bake for 35–40 minutes, until golden and bubbling. Serve with lemon wedges.

MOROCCAN CHICKPEA & NOODLE SOUP

✳✳✳ When I was growing up, our neighbors were Moroccan and we were often invited to
✳✳✳ share a bowl of *harira* with them. Eventually I started making it for myself. I always use
organic ingredients and it makes a delicious and substantial meal. We eat it with chopped
dates – that doesn't sound like it should work, but it does! Make sure that all your stirring is
done with love and prayer.

SERVES 4-6

2 onions, roughly chopped
4 celery sticks, chopped
1 (400g/14.5 oz) can
     chopped tomatoes
25g/1¼ cups cilantro
20g/1 cup fresh parsley
1 tsp ground black pepper
½ tsp ground white pepper
½ tsp ground turmeric
1 cinnamon stick
1 tsp ground ginger
1½ tsp salt (see note)
1½ tsp olive oil
1 liter/1 quart boiling water
½ (420g/15.5 oz) can
     chickpeas, rinsed and
     loose skins removed
35g/⅓ cup brown rice
     vermicelli noodles,
     crushed by hand
1 heaping tbsp whole-wheat
     flour
1 egg, beaten
½ tsp *smen* (see note) or
     1 tsp ghee
handful of dates, chopped
Khobz (page 92) or a bread of
     your choice, to serve
1 lemon, cut into wedges

Place the onions, celery, tomatoes, cilantro and parsley in a food
processor and process until smooth. Pour the pureed ingredients
into a large pot. Add the spices, salt and olive oil and bring to a boil,
then simmer for about 15 minutes, stirring occasionally.

Add the boiling water, turn up the heat and boil for 20–25 minutes,
until the liquid has reduced and thickened.

Add the chickpeas and noodles, turn the heat to low and simmer
for 5 minutes.

Mix the flour with 2–3 tablespoons of water to make a soft paste.
Turn up the heat and when the mixture starts to boil, whisk the
flour paste into the soup until well blended.

Whisk the egg into the soup along with the *smen* or ghee, whisking
all the time. Turn the heat to the lowest setting and simmer for
5 minutes.

Serve the soup in bowls, garnished with chopped dates, with bread
and, if you like, lemon wedges to squeeze in.

NOTES I like to use pink Himalayan salt, but you can use regular
salt if you wish.

Smen is Moroccan fermented butter and can be found in Middle
Eastern stores or online.

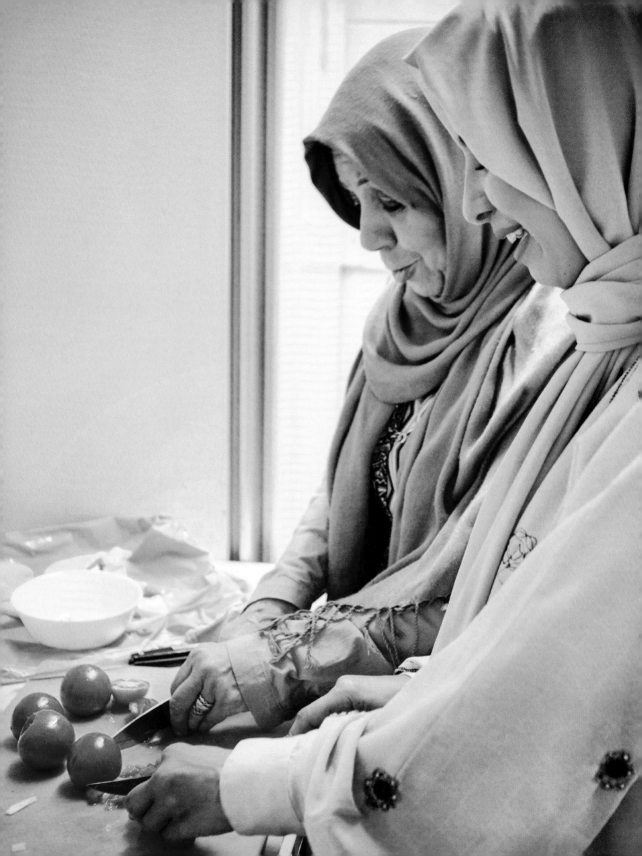

SALADS
AND
SIDES

FATTOUSH SALAD

Fattoush is a classic in Arab cooking. Sumac gives it authentic flavor and isn't hard to find. I came to the UK in 1989 and even back then it was easy to get all the ingredients I needed to cook recipes from home. Now, with the internet, you can order anything you need online.

SERVES 4 AS A MAIN OR 6 AS A SIDE

2 pita breads

7 tbsp extra-virgin olive oil

3 ripe tomatoes, quartered and cut into 1cm/½-in wedges

1 small cucumber, about 175g/6 oz, halved lengthwise and cut into 1cm/½-in slices

½ green pepper, cored, seeded and finely chopped

20 large red radishes, trimmed and quartered

2 heads little gem lettuce, cored and roughly chopped

3 scallions, finely chopped

3 tbsp finely chopped parsley (optional)

1 tbsp finely chopped mint

juice of ½ lemon

2 tbsp pomegranate molasses

good pinch of sumac (optional; see note)

salt and pepper

Preheat the oven to 400°F. Line a baking sheet with parchment paper.

Split the pitas in half horizontally, then tear each half into 2cm/¾-inch pieces. Place in a bowl, add 2 tablespoons of the olive oil and salt and pepper to taste; toss to combine. Spread on the baking sheet and bake for about 10 minutes, until golden and crisp. Set aside.

Place the chopped vegetables in a salad bowl, and add the scallions and chopped herbs.

Season with lemon juice, pomegranate molasses, salt and pepper and toss well. Drizzle with the remaining 5 tablespoons olive oil and toss again.

Top the salad with the crispy pita, sprinkle with sumac and serve immediately.

NOTE Sumac is a spice with a red color and a lemony flavor; it is sold in Middle Eastern food shops, large supermarkets and online.

YEMENI BREAD

The smell of this baking takes me back to our little village in Yemen. It's the traditional bread my mum used to make when I was growing up. It's what my son calls *"gida cooking,"* which is Yemeni for "grandma cooking." You can eat it with butter or jam, but back home we had it with olives and dipped in sesame oil.

SERVES 4-6

475g/3⅓ cups bread flour, plus extra for dusting

1 tsp salt

1 heaping tsp fast-acting dried yeast (half of a 7g package)

275ml/1 cup plus 2 tbsp warm water

1½ tsp olive oil, plus extra for oiling

Put the flour and salt in a large bowl. Mix to combine, then make a hollow in the center. Add the yeast to the hollow with a splash of the warm water and mix with your fingertips to help dissolve the yeast. Once dissolved, continue to gradually add the water and combine all the ingredients to form a sticky dough. Cover the bowl with three clean kitchen towels and let rest in a warm place for 5 minutes.

Lightly oil two baking sheets. Turn the dough out onto a lightly floured surface and knead for 10 minutes, until smooth. Divide into three pieces (about 250g/9 oz each), then knead each piece of dough for 1 minute and roll into a smooth ball. Transfer two balls to one baking sheet, and the third to the second sheet. Cover with kitchen towels and let rest for 10 minutes.

Preheat the oven to 400°F.

Using your hands or a rolling pin, flatten each dough ball to form a 15cm/6-inch disk, no more than 2cm/¾-inch thick. Cover and let rest for 15 minutes.

Brush each disk with the olive oil and prick four times with a fork. Transfer to the oven and bake for 10 minutes, then rotate the baking sheets so the bread colors evenly and bake for a final 10 minutes. Serve warm, with mint tea, butter and jam.

SALAD SHIRAZI

 This is a simple salad, with just a few ingredients, from the south of Iran. The fresh flavors go well with chicken or with lamb dishes such as *Ghormeh Sabzi* (see page 57).

SERVES 4

3 small Persian cucumbers, 350g/12 oz, diced

3 tomatoes, 300g/10 oz, seeded and diced

¼ red onion, finely diced

zest and juice of 1 lime

¼ tsp salt

¼ tsp ground black pepper

2 tbsp olive oil

Mix the diced cucumber, tomato and onion in a serving bowl.

Add the lime zest and juice, salt, pepper and olive oil. Toss gently until all the ingredients are well coated and serve immediately.

NOTE Persian cucumbers are supposed to be less bitter, but it is fine to use regular ones. You can also use lemon zest and juice in place of the lime, if desired.

COLESLAW

 I discovered this recipe when visiting Syria ten years ago. If you've never thought of adding red pepper flakes to coleslaw, you'll be amazed – it really wakes up the flavor.

SERVES 4

2 carrots, coarsely grated

400g/14 oz green cabbage, sliced

½ red pepper, finely diced

25g/1¼ cups cilantro, chopped

3 tbsp mayonnaise

7 tbsp plain yogurt

¼ tsp ground black pepper

¼ tsp red pepper flakes

salt

Place all the ingredients in a large serving bowl and toss well, with love and care, to combine. Taste and adjust the seasoning if necessary and chill in the fridge for at least 1 hour before serving.

TABBOULEH

 In Arab cooking, we always have pickles and olives on the table, and every meal needs something green. More often than not, it's tabbouleh.

SERVES 4

40g/¼ cup bulgur wheat

75ml/5 tbsp boiling water

100g/5 cups parsley,
   chopped

10g/½ cup mint leaves,
   finely chopped

2 scallions, thinly sliced

⅓ cucumber, peeled, seeded
   and finely chopped

200g/1¼ cups cherry
   tomatoes: 150g/1 cup
   finely chopped,
   50g/¼ cup left whole

40g/⅓ cup pitted green
   olives

For the dressing

¼ cup olive oil

juice of 1½ lemons

2 tbsp pomegranate
   molasses

salt and pepper

Put the bulgur wheat in a small bowl, add the boiling water, then immediately cover tightly with foil and place a kitchen towel on top. Let steam for 20 minutes.

To make the dressing, mix the oil, lemon juice and pomegranate molasses with a pinch of salt and pepper.

Using a fork, fluff up the bulgur wheat (don't worry if there is a little liquid left) then transfer to a large bowl. Add the parsley, mint, scallions, cucumber and chopped tomatoes and a pinch of salt and pepper. Mix to combine; taste and adjust the seasoning if necessary. Add half the dressing and mix well; taste and add the remaining dressing if you like.

Serve in a dish with the whole tomatoes and olives on top.

RAINBOW ROASTED VEGETABLES

To me, the way the table looks is as important as how the food tastes. I make sure there are always flowers on the tables at Al-Manaar. And I make this dish often because it adds beautiful color to any meal.

SERVES 4-6

250g/9 oz purple or yellow potatoes, cut into wedges

200g/7 oz each beets and golden beets, peeled and cut into thin wedges

350g/12 oz kabocha or butternut squash, seeded and cut into 2cm/¾-in wedges

120g/4¼ oz baby carrots, or regular carrots, peeled and cut into chunks

175g/6 oz baby parsnips, halved, or regular parsnips, peeled and cut into chunks

4 tbsp extra-virgin olive oil

½ tsp red pepper flakes

2 tsp dried oregano

2 small red and/or yellow peppers, seeded, cut into chunks or rings

1 zucchini, sliced

150g/5¼ oz Brussels sprouts, halved

1 watermelon radish, halved and sliced, or 120g/4¼ oz daikon radishes, cut into 3cm/1¼-in slices

12 asparagus tips

salt and pepper

Preheat the oven to 425°F. You will need two large baking sheets; the vegetables need to be baked separately because of their different cooking times.

Arrange the potatoes, beets, squash, carrots and parsnips on one of the baking sheets, in a single layer. Drizzle with 1½ tablespoons of olive oil, sprinkle with half the red pepper flakes and oregano and season with salt and pepper. Roast on the top rack of the oven for 20 minutes.

Arrange the rest of the vegetables on the second baking sheet in a single layer, drizzle with the remaining olive oil, sprinkle with the remaining red pepper flakes and oregano and season with salt and pepper.

When the first baking sheet of vegetables has cooked for 20–25 minutes, move it to the middle rack and place the second baking sheet on the top rack. Roast both sheets for 20–25 minutes, or until all the vegetables are tender but not mushy.

Tip all the vegetables into a serving dish, taste and adjust the seasoning and serve.

NOTE If you want the vegetables to be more charred, remove from the oven after 10–15 minutes and place each baking sheet under the broiler for a few minutes, watching carefully to make sure the vegetables don't burn.

FENNEL & ORANGE SALAD

I never liked fennel until I lived in Italy and tasted it raw in this salad. It's Sicilian in origin and you can use blood oranges when in season, for both taste and color. You can replace the fennel with peeled, thinly sliced raw beets for an equally delicious salad. *Buon appetito!*

SERVES 4

2 fennel bulbs, about
  600g/1⅓ lb
2 large oranges
2 tbsp raisins (optional)
1 tsp cider vinegar
5 tbsp extra-virgin olive oil
3 tbsp pine nuts, toasted
  (see page 127)
1 tbsp pumpkin seeds
salt

Trim the fennel bulbs, discarding the bases, cores and any tough outer layers. Cut the tops off and reserve any feathery fronds. Cut each bulb in half from top to bottom and place flat side down on a chopping board. Using a sharp knife (or a mandolin), slice the fennel as thinly as possible. Transfer to a bowl of iced water until ready to serve. This will prevent browning and make it crisper.

Squeeze one orange and place the juice in a small bowl. Add the raisins, if using, and let soak for at least 10 minutes. If you're not using raisins, keep the juice for the dressing.

Peel the other orange and cut into thin slices. (You can remove the pith, but remember that it is good for you.) Set aside.

Remove the raisins from the orange juice and set aside. Add a pinch of salt and the vinegar to the juice, then gradually whisk in the olive oil.

Place the fennel, reserved fronds, orange slices, raisins, pine nuts and pumpkin seeds in a salad bowl. Add the dressing, toss gently and serve.

LILLIAN OLWA'S

CARROT & ONION CHAPATIS

I was never a keen cook, but I got so fed up with the takeout we've been eating while living in temporary accommodation that I found myself craving home-cooked food and the tastes I had grown up with in Uganda. I started cooking my mum's recipes and then began experimenting with my own, like this one. The Hubb Community Kitchen has been a haven for me – and it has revived my love of food.

MAKES 8 CHAPATIS

2 large carrots, grated
300g/2 cups plus 2 tbsp
    all-purpose flour, plus
    extra for dusting
½ small onion, grated
½ tsp salt
5 tbsp vegetable oil
3 tbsp melted ghee, or extra
    vegetable oil, for brushing

Squeeze the grated carrots between your hands to remove the juice. Reserve the juice in a small bowl.

Place the flour in a large bowl. Add the carrots, grated onion and onion juices, salt and oil and mix to form a soft dough. Add a little of the reserved carrot juice if needed.

Knead the dough for 10 minutes, until elastic and smooth. Rub the dough with a little oil and place in a plastic bag. Set aside for about 1 hour.

Divide the dough into eight balls. Sprinkle a little flour on the work surface and roll each ball into a 17cm/6½-inch round.

Heat a frying pan over medium-low heat. Dry cook each chapati for about 1 minute, until it starts to brown, then flip and cook for another 1 minute. When the chapati starts to puff up, press down with a rolled kitchen towel to force the steam to escape, rotating them at the same time to avoid excessive browning. Once cooked, lightly brush both sides with ghee or oil, wrap in a kitchen towel and keep warm until ready to serve.

DESSERTS
AND
DRINKS

CARAMELIZED PLUM UPSIDE-DOWN CAKE

✳✳✳ As soon as I heard about the Kitchen, I volunteered to help, cooking recipes from my
✳✳✳ homeland, Algeria. This cake is one my mum used to make. She always said plums are
an unreliable fruit – they can be quite sour when raw. This brings out the best in them.

SERVES 8-10

2 tsp sunflower oil,
    for greasing
300g/1½ cups granulated
    sugar
100g/7 tbsp unsalted butter,
    at room temperature
½ tsp vanilla extract
¼ tsp salt
8 plums, halved and pitted
40g/¼ packed cup dark
    brown sugar
2 eggs
2 heaping tbsp cornstarch
50g/⅓ cup plus 1 tbsp
    almond meal
100g/¾ cup all-purpose
    flour
1 tsp baking powder

Preheat the oven to 375°F. Grease a 23cm/9-inch round springform cake pan with sunflower oil and place on a baking sheet.

For the caramel, put 225g/1 cup plus 2 tablespoons of the granulated sugar into a small, wide, heavy pan over low heat. Without stirring, let the sugar dissolve completely. Once liquid, let it gently bubble for 15–20 minutes, until it is a deep golden color. Add 1 tablespoon of the butter, half the vanilla extract and the salt, gently swirling the pan to combine the butter as it melts. Once fully incorporated, immediately remove from the heat and pour the caramel into the prepared cake pan. Place the plum halves on top, cut side down, nestled tightly together, and set aside.

In a large bowl, beat the remaining 85g/6 tablespoons butter together with the remaining 75g/6 tablespoons granulated sugar and the brown sugar until pale and creamy: this will take 2–3 minutes using electric beaters; if you don't have them, use a wooden spoon. Add the eggs one at a time, beating well. Once the eggs are well combined, add the remaining vanilla extract, the cornstarch, almond meal, flour and baking powder to the bowl and fold through with a spoon until just combined (taking care not to overmix), then pour over the plums. Smooth the top, then bake for 50–55 minutes until cooked through; a thin skewer inserted in the center should come out clean.

Transfer the cake to a wire rack and let cool in the pan for 5 minutes. Place a serving plate on top of the pan and flip over before releasing the sides of the pan and removing the base. Let the cake cool for another 5 minutes before slicing.

AYSHA BORA'S *Nankhatai*

INDIAN SHORTBREAD

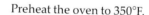 We're all foodies in my family. I have four daughters, ranging in age from five to fifteen, and we all eat together as a family every evening, sitting on the floor, talking about our day. You can serve these biscuits for breakfast, afternoon tea, or as dessert. They keep for days in an airtight container.

MAKES 35 BISCUITS

120g/½ cup ghee

120g/1 cup confectioners' sugar

2 tbsp plain yogurt

160g/1 cup plus 2 tbsp all-purpose flour

35g/5 tbsp chickpea flour

seeds from 4 cardamom pods, coarsely ground

½ tsp baking powder

2 tbsp shelled pistachios, blitzed in a spice grinder or food processor

Line two baking sheets with parchment paper.

Put the ghee and sugar into a food processor and blitz until combined, about 10 seconds. Add the yogurt and blitz again, then set aside for 10 minutes.

Meanwhile, sift the flours, cardamom and baking powder into a mixing bowl. Add the flour mixture to the food processor. Pulse briefly until combined, then return the mixture to the bowl.

Using your hands, make 35 balls, about 15g/½ oz each. Place the balls on the baking sheets, spaced well apart. Put the baking sheets in the fridge to chill for 20 minutes.

Preheat the oven to 350°F.

Remove the baking sheets from the fridge and bake on the middle and lower racks of the oven for 13–15 minutes, rotating the baking sheets halfway through.

Remove from the oven and immediately sprinkle the pistachios on top. Let cool on the baking sheets for 10 minutes, then transfer the shortbreads to a wire rack to cool completely.

CARDAMOM BREAD & BUTTER PUDDING

When I started visiting the Hubb Kitchen, it motivated me to cook much more. My Mum is my inspiration. She was taught by her mother, but she adds her own little touches and she invented this dessert for us when I was a child. Now I make it too. My little boy is six and he loves his food; I think that's thanks to her.

SERVES 4-6

6 thick slices of white bread
225g/1 cup unsalted butter
800ml/3⅓ cups whole milk
150g/¾ cup sugar
¼ tsp ground cardamom
250ml/1 cup heavy cream
toasted sliced almonds,
   to serve (see page 127)

Cut the bread slices in half diagonally.

Melt the butter in a small pan. Dip the pieces of bread in the butter to coat both sides, then toast, in batches, in a large pan over medium heat for 2–4 minutes on each side, until golden. Arrange the bread in a serving dish.

Put the milk, sugar and cardamom in a pot and bring to a boil, then simmer for 10 minutes. Let cool for 5 minutes.

Pour the spiced milk over the bread. Gently press the bread into the milk. Set aside for 1 hour, pressing occasionally, until all the milk has been absorbed.

Pour the cream over the top, sprinkle with the sliced almonds, cover with plastic wrap and chill in the fridge for at least 30 minutes before serving.

TOFFEE-APPLE CRUMBLE

When the mosque offered the kitchen to the community, I would come by and help out. It gives ladies a place to relax, make some home-cooked food and have a good girly catch-up. I'm not much of a one for making desserts, but I do enjoy them. This is a random concoction that I made up – it's quick and easy … I like that!

SERVES 4-6

4 large Granny Smith apples
200g/¾ cup plus 2 tbsp
    unsalted butter, chilled
    and cut into small cubes
175g/1 packed cup brown
    sugar
120ml/½ cup heavy cream
large pinch of salt
150g/1 cup plus 1 tbsp
    all-purpose flour

Preheat the oven to 400°C.

Peel and core the apples and cut into 3cm/1-inch pieces. Place in a medium pan with 2 tablespoons of water, cover and cook over medium heat for 5–6 minutes, until just soft at the edges. Transfer to a 25 x 20cm/8-inch-square baking dish. Set aside.

Place half of the butter cubes and half of the brown sugar in a heavy pan over low heat for 2 minutes, until the sugar has dissolved. Increase the heat to medium and let bubble for 5–6 minutes, stirring occasionally, until the mixture is a dark toffee color. Add the cream and salt, taking care as it will splatter, then stir until well blended. Pour the caramel over the apples and stir to coat all the pieces.

Place the flour and the remaining butter (ensuring it is very cold) in a bowl. Using your fingertips, rub the butter into the flour until the mixture looks like coarse breadcrumbs. Add the remaining sugar and toss until well blended. Sprinkle the crumble over the apple mixture.

Bake for 30–35 minutes, until the top is golden and the caramel is bubbling at the edges. Leave to cool slightly before serving.

SWEET PUFF PASTRIES

I like to make most things from scratch but when it comes to puff pastry, store-bought is so much quicker and easier. If you keep a pack in the freezer, you can make these pretty rose-scented pastries whenever visitors turn up.

MAKES ABOUT 15 PASTRIES

250ml/1 cup whole milk

3 tbsp cornstarch

2 tbsp sugar

3 tbsp heavy cream

3 tbsp rose water or
   ½ tsp vanilla extract

120g/4½ oz cream cheese,
   at room temperature

320g/11 oz store-bought
   puff pastry, thawed in the
   fridge overnight

1 egg, beaten

5 tbsp honey, or to taste

1 tbsp black sesame seeds or
   finely chopped pistachios

Put the milk, cornstarch and sugar in a small pan and stir until the cornstarch has dissolved. Heat the mixture over medium heat for a couple of minutes, stirring all the time and more vigorously as it thickens. Remove from the heat, stir in the cream, rose water or vanilla, and cream cheese, and leave to cool for 30 minutes.

Preheat the oven to 425°F. Line a baking sheet with parchment paper.

Unroll the puff pastry and cut into squares (about 7cm/3 inches). Place a small amount of the cream cheese mixture on one corner of each square, then fold the other corner over to make a triangle. Seal the parcels by gently pressing the edges with the tines of a fork. Brush the tops with beaten egg and bake for 15–20 minutes, until puffed and golden.

While the puffs are still warm, drizzle with honey and sprinkle with black sesame seeds or pistachios. Serve warm or cold.

RUSSIAN SEMOLINA CAKE

Kefir is an ingredient that originated in the Caucasus Mountains. It's fermented milk – a bit like yogurt but with a slight fizz to it – and has great health benefits, so it is now being stocked in supermarkets and health food stores. As a drink it's an acquired taste, but in this traditional cake it just adds an edge to the sweetness.

SERVES 4-6

190g/1 cup plus 2 tbsp
   coarse semolina
250g/1 cup kefir
100g/7 tbsp unsalted butter,
   at room temperature, plus
   extra for greasing
¼ tsp salt
160g/¾ packed cup plus
   2 tbsp dark brown sugar
½ tsp vanilla bean paste
2 eggs
1 tsp baking soda
condensed milk, to serve
   (optional)

Place the semolina and kefir in a bowl and mix until well blended. Cover with a clean kitchen towel and set aside for 2 hours.

Preheat the oven to 400°F. Butter a 20cm/8-inch or 9-inch round cake pan.

Using a handheld electric mixer, beat the butter until soft. Add the salt and brown sugar and beat until creamy and slightly lighter in color. Add the vanilla and then the eggs, one at a time, beating thoroughly after each addition.

Gradually incorporate the semolina mixture, then the baking soda, beating well after each addition. Pour the batter into the cake pan and bake for 35–40 minutes, until brown and springy to the touch. Let cool in the pan.

Slice and serve, drizzled with condensed milk if using.

CHERINE MALLAH'S *Atayef*

RICOTTA-FILLED PANCAKES WITH ORANGE BLOSSOM SYRUP

These pancakes are filled with a mixture of ricotta, orange blossom syrup and crushed pistachios and they are a traditional dessert often served at Ramadan. However, we like to eat them all year round, as they are also very light and lower in fat than most desserts.

MAKES 12 PANCAKES

For the batter
150g/¾ cup plus 2 tbsp fine semolina
75g/⅔ cup self-rising flour
1 heaping tsp fast-acting dried yeast (half of a 7g package)
½ tsp baking powder
1 tsp sugar
pinch of salt
375ml/1½ cups warm water

For the syrup
100g/½ cup sugar
125ml/½ cup water
2 tbsp orange blossom water

For the filling
250g/1 cup ricotta
2 tbsp shelled pistachios, crushed

Put all the ingredients for the batter in a large bowl and whisk to thoroughly combine. Cover loosely with plastic wrap and set aside to rise for 45 minutes.

Meanwhile, make the syrup. Heat the sugar, water and orange blossom water in a small pan over low heat until the sugar has dissolved, about 5 minutes. Increase the heat and boil for about 10 minutes, until the mixture reaches a syrup consistency. Transfer to a small bowl and let cool.

Heat a non-stick pan over medium-low heat; when it's hot, add a small ladleful of batter to the pan. Cook the pancake for 3–4 minutes, until the surface has lots of bubbles and has dried. Do not flip; transfer straight to paper towels and repeat with the rest of the batter, making a total of 12 pancakes. Set aside, but do not stack them or they may stick together.

When you have made all the pancakes, prepare the filling. Mix the ricotta with 3 tablespoons of the cooled syrup. Hold one pancake in the palm of your hand and add 1 tablespoon of the ricotta mixture to the center. Bring the edges of the pancake together and press firmly to seal the pancake until you reach the center – leaving half the pancake open. Sprinkle some of the crushed pistachios on the exposed ricotta filling and set aside. Fill the remaining pancakes in the same way.

Serve with the remaining syrup alongside.

SIMPLE CHOCOLATE CAKE

I got this recipe from my sister Linda, who lives in France. It's a family favorite and was one of the first things I brought in when I started coming to the Kitchen. Then I kept getting messages from the women saying "bring more chocolate cake next time." It's very easy and always works. If I'm in a hurry I don't always bother with icing, but if you do, it's special enough for a birthday cake. I decorate it with chocolate buttons and little cookies for the kids and they love it.

SERVES 6-8
125g/4½ oz dark chocolate, finely chopped
3 tbsp whole milk
125g/1 cup self-rising flour
¼ tsp salt
3 tbsp cocoa powder
150g/10 tbsp unsalted butter, at room temperature, plus extra for greasing
150g/¾ cup granulated sugar
3 eggs

For the icing
75g/5 tbsp unsalted butter, at room temperature
1 tbsp heavy cream
1 tsp vanilla extract
175g/1½ cups confectioners' sugar
1 tbsp cocoa powder, plus extra for sprinkling

Preheat the oven to 300°F. Butter a 20cm/8-inch or 9-inch round cake pan and line with parchment paper.

Place the chocolate and milk in a heatproof bowl and set over a pan of barely simmering water, ensuring that the bottom of the bowl does not touch the water. Once melted, let cool slightly.

Sift the flour, salt and cocoa powder together. Set aside.

Using a handheld electric mixer, beat the butter until soft. Add the granulated sugar and beat until creamy and light. Add the eggs one at a time, beating thoroughly after each addition.

Using a rubber spatula, fold in the melted chocolate and then the flour and cocoa mixture until just combined, without overworking the batter. Pour into the prepared pan, smooth the top and bake for 35–40 minutes, until a skewer inserted in the center comes out clean. Let cool completely in the pan, before turning out.

To make the icing, mix the butter together with the cream and vanilla, then gradually add the confectioners' sugar and cocoa powder, mixing until the icing is soft and fluffy.

Spread the icing on top of the cake and sprinkle lightly with cocoa powder. Alternatively, you can slice the cake in half horizontally and sandwich the two halves together with half of the icing, then spread the rest on top.

MASALA CHAI

 This cinnamon-flavored tea is an infusion of many flavors and has many health benefits. It is a much-loved treat, especially in Pakistan and India.

SERVES 4

2-cm/¾-in piece fresh ginger
6 green cardamom pods
700ml/3 cups water
300ml/1¼ cups whole milk
1 cinnamon stick
¼ tsp ground black pepper
2 tbsp loose black tea leaves
2 tbsp sugar, or to taste

Peel and chop the ginger and slightly crush the cardamom pods under the blade of a knife.

Put the water, milk, ginger and spices in a pan. Bring to a boil, reduce the heat and simmer for 10 minutes, stirring all the time to prevent the milk from boiling over.

Add the tea leaves and sugar, stir and simmer for another 5 minutes.

Strain into mugs or heatproof glasses and serve.

MUNIRA MAHMUD'S

GINGER TEA

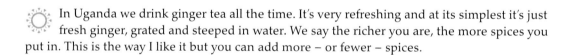 In Uganda we drink ginger tea all the time. It's very refreshing and at its simplest it's just fresh ginger, grated and steeped in water. We say the richer you are, the more spices you put in. This is the way I like it but you can add more – or fewer – spices.

SERVES 4

7-cm/2¾-in piece fresh
    ginger
6 green cardamom pods
1 cinnamon stick
¼ tsp ground black pepper
5 cloves
1 star anise
800ml/3⅓ cups water
sugar to taste

Peel and grate the ginger and slightly crush the cardamom pods under the blade of a knife.

Place all the spices in a pan and cover with the water. Bring to a boil, reduce the heat and simmer for 15 minutes.

Strain into mugs or heatproof glasses, add sugar to taste and serve.

SPICED MINT TEA

This reminds me of my dad. We used to have it in little glasses with gold rims, and he would lift the pot up and down as he poured so we could see the pale green tea streaming out. I don't put a lot of sugar in my version, but Dad drank his honey-sweet! *Pictured on page 121.*

SERVES 4

15g/¾ cup fresh mint

1 clove

1 cinnamon stick

½ tsp sugar (optional)

700ml/3 cups boiling water

Place the mint and spices (and sugar if using) in a teapot and pour in the boiling water. Let infuse for 5 minutes, then serve in small tea cups or heatproof glasses.

INDEX

THE ROYAL FOUNDATION

Together has been created with help from The Royal Foundation, which is the primary philanthropic and charitable vehicle for The Duke and Duchess of Cambridge and The Duke and Duchess of Sussex.

The work of The Royal Foundation is driven by a desire to make a difference together. The charity focuses on bringing people together and developing innovative projects that will bring lasting change around issues that matter to society, and which Their Royal Highnesses are passionate about.

The Duchess of Sussex and The Royal Foundation have worked with the women of the Hubb Community Kitchen since early 2018 to create *Together*.

A portion of the proceeds from the sales of this book will support the Hubb Community Kitchen in London, keeping it open for up to seven days a week, helping widen its reach to others in the community, and enabling it to continue transforming lives through the power of cooking.

The Royal Foundation is administering the transfer of funds from the sale of *Together* to the Hubb Community Kitchen.

For more information about the kitchen please visit:

www.royalfoundation.com/together-cookbook